SCHOLASTIC

Book of

FIRSTS

JAMES BUCKLEY, JR.

SCHOLASTIC REFERENCE
an imprint of
SCHOLASTIC

Produced by Shoreline Publishing Group LLC
Santa Barbara, California
www.shorelinepublishing.com
President/Editorial Director: James Buckley, Jr.
Designed by Tom Carling, Carling Design Inc.
Illustrations by David Sheldon and Robert Prince
Additional editorial help was provided by David Fischer (sports), Phil Barber (food, exploration),
Michael Burgan (George Washington), and Michael Teitelbaum (Jackie Robinson).
Editing and proofreading assistance came from Beth Adelman and Michelle Drown.
Index was created by Nanette Cardon, IRIS.

Thanks to Ken Wright and Elysa Jacobs at Scholastic Reference, who are "first" in our hearts
among great editors to work with. Plus a bonus thanks for Paula Manzanero for coming in
from the bull pen for the save!

Library of Congress Cataloging-in-Publication Data is available.

0-439-67607-X

10 9 8 7 6 5 4 3 2   05 06 07 08 09

Printed in the U.S.A.
First printing, June 2005

Table of Contents

First Things First

There's a very old riddle that asks this question: Which came first, the chicken or the egg? Well, if it was the chicken, then where did it come from, since chickens hatch from eggs. If it was the egg, then where did it come from, since eggs have to be laid by—that's right—chickens. It's a bit of a puzzle—with no right answer.

So, how do you decide if something came first? Fortunately, it's not always as difficult as the chicken-and-egg thing. In this book, you'll find more than 1,000 people or things that really did come first. We've combed the books and archives of the world (okay, the libraries and the Internet) to track down the stories behind some of the most important firsts in history.

Why is it important to know who or what came first? That's another good question and one that's easier to answer than that poultry puzzler. In just about any subject we humans find ourselves interested in, it's very useful to know how something started, what steps led to its invention, or who blazed the trail. Knowing who was first gives us a leg up on continuing the work they started. Sometimes, knowing what led to a discovery helps future researchers discover more firsts. And, of course, knowing where things come from is just pretty cool information to have in your brain. You know when your first birthday was, don't you? Or where your first house was? Or the name of your first school? Knowing firsts like these helps us to understand who we are now—and where we're going.

So, what can you find in this book? First, lots and lots of people who did things first. The first person to fly faster than the speed of sound . . . the first person to invent an automatic dishwasher . . . the first kid to win an Academy Award . . . the first American woman to become a police officer . . . and many, many more.

Being the first to do something can sometimes take bravery (such as Sir Edmund Hillary and Tenzing Norgay, the first people to climb Mt. Everest, page 113) or luck (such as Percy Spencer, whose surprise first can be found on page 120). It can take years of hard work (the first steam railroad train, page 308) or just a moment of inspiration (such as the discovery of X-rays by Wihelm Roentgen, page 197). Firsts of every description and origin are inside.

Plus, along with lists of firsts, you'll find some longer stories in this book about very important first people. Among them are the first president of the United States, George Washington; the first doctor to perform a heart transplant, Christiaan Barnard; the men who

What's Your First _____ ?

You've had dozens of firsts throughout your life, from your first birthday to the first time you lost a tooth. Throughout this book, we've created lots of places for you to record those personal firsts. Your first trip to the doctor . . . the first time you rode a bike . . . the first time you cooked a meal by yourself . . . your first teacher . . . and many more. See if you can think of some "me firsts" that we haven't thought of!

built the first airplane, Orville and Wilbur Wright; the first African-American baseball player in the major leagues, Jackie Robinson; and many others.

But fun firsts aren't just about people. The things we use in our lives had to start somewhere, and their stories are in here, too (we've even got animal firsts on page 158). The first toaster, the first paper money, the first hockey goalie mask, the first subway, the first video game, etc. The Everyday Things, Technology, and Transportation chapters, for instance, detail numerous important firsts that have changed the way people live their lives. Without the first car, television, computer, lightbulb, or e-mail, modern life would be way, way different!

And just in case you think that all the good firsts have been taken, don't worry. New firsts are being made all the time. In June 2004, the first privately funded aircraft, called *SpaceShipOne*, reached outer space. In the same month, the first official presidential portrait painted by an African-American artist (Simmie Knox's portrayal of Bill Clinton) was unveiled at the White House.

Of course, we're still waiting for the first woman U.S. president, the first brain transplant, and the first astronaut to land on Mars. So you've got a shot at being in a future edition of this book!

New or old, modern or ancient, brave or lucky—whatever path a person or a thing took to become a first, you'll find out about it inside. Be the first in your class to read this book! But even if you're not, you can always make this the first time you've read the book, so that's a first all by itself.

SAY IT FIRST...

Another thing to look for in this book are the "Say It First..." boxes. The word "first" is used in many phrases, and we've highlighted some of them in this book. What kinds of food are served as a first course? What sport uses a first down? What does first aid mean? How can you tell if you're holding a first edition in your hands right now? Look for the answers to all of those questions and more inside this book.

Where Did We Find All This Stuff?!

We've got a surprise for you: This is NOT the first book of firsts! Many writers over the years have created books, Web sites, newspaper and magazine articles, and more, documenting firsts. Their hard work was a big part of our research for creating the *Scholastic Book of Firsts*. We've got more than 1,000 firsts in this book, but there are thousands more out there for you to discover. Your librarian or teacher can guide you to some other books of firsts. Keep searching, because each time you discover something in one of these books, it becomes the first time you learned that fact!

Abbreviations Used in This Book

Some of the entries in this book contain abbreviations, usually for measurements. (For example: How far did Charles Lindbergh fly when he became the first solo pilot to cross the Atlantic Ocean? Check out page 17 to find out.) We're using both the "regular" American system (feet, pounds, miles, etc.) and the metric system (meters, liters, etc.). Here's a list of the abbreviations you'll see and what they mean:

ft.	foot or feet	m	meter
kg	kilogram	sq. km	square kilometer
km	kilometer	sq. mi.	square mile
lb.	pound	C	Celsius
		F	Farenheit

CHAPTER 1

Air & Space

Look, up in the sky!
It's, it's . . . there's all sorts of stuff up there!
Read on to discover gravity-breaking firsts.

Balloons, Zeppelins,

The dream of flight has been around as long as human beings have watched birds soar in the sky. Before the invention of engines that could power craft into the air, inventive people got a lift from the air itself. Knowing that hot air rises, they created bags to hold the hot air. The bags would rise, and bingo...flight.

The First Balloons

After several inventors built small hot-air balloons, a pair of French brothers were the first to carry creatures in them. In 1783, Joseph and Étienne Montgolfier sent a balloon more than 1,000 feet (305 m) in the air. A small fire of wood shavings created the hot air that filled the balloon. Their second attempt carried a duck, a rooster, and a sheep. On October 15, 1783, François Pilâtre de Rozier used his own balloon to become the first human to fly in an aircraft.

At the same time, Jacques A. C. Charles created the first balloon filled with the gas hydrogen. Hydrogen gas is lighter than air. Fill a balloon with it and the balloon rises. Release the gas and the balloon sinks. Hydrogen soon proved to be more efficient than hot air—the ballooning age had begun. In January 1785, a hydrogen balloon became the first aircraft to cross the English Channel.

In January 1793, our first president, George Washington, watched the first balloon flight in America. Frenchman Jean-Pierre Blanchard flew for 46 minutes above Philadelphia.

The First Zeppelins

Balloons were nice, but they were hard to steer and they could only go as fast as the wind carried them. In 1894, German Count Ferdinand von Zeppelin built an airship that solved those problems. He covered a large aluminum frame with cloth and then filled it with hydrogen. The frame allowed

and Gliders

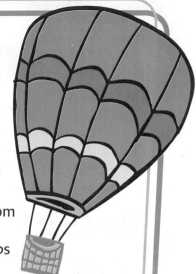

him to mount propellers, driven by motors, beneath the giant bag of gas. Zeppelins could be steered in different directions and change speeds more easily than balloons. By 1912, zeppelins became the first aircraft to carry passengers on regular routes, to and from cities in Germany.

Even as airplanes became popular, airships like these remained in use until the 1930s.

The First Gliders

Another way early aviators took to the sky was on gliders. These large, airplane-like craft had no power, but could ride the winds and then land safely. In 1893, German pilot Otto Lilienthal became the first person to take off, fly, and safely land a glider. Many of the lessons he learned while floating like a bird were later used by the Wright brothers in making their airplanes (see page 12).

First Fliers?

The mythical King Bladud of England, who supposedly founded the city of Bath, England, was also a would-be aviator. According to legend, he built giant wings made of wood and feathers and tried to fly by jumping off a tower. Not surprisingly, he was unsuccessful. Also, a Greek myth tells the story of the inventor Daedalus and his son Icarus. They built wings of feathers held together by wax. Though warned not to, Icarus flew too close to the sun, the wax melted, and, well, gravity took over.

IN THE FIRST PLACE...

The Wright Brothers

A pair of brothers from Dayton, Ohio, literally changed the world. Before Orville and Wilbur Wright unlocked the secrets of flight, human beings were stuck on the ground. It took many weeks to travel great distances. The only way to cross an ocean was on a ship. No one besides slow-moving balloonists had seen Earth from the sky.

The Wright brothers ran a bicycle shop in Dayton. Their interest in mechanical things and motion led them to study flying. They read books and articles, studied the research done by many others, and started making plans and models of aircraft. They soon understood that the key to flight was control.

For a century, engineers had been looking for an aircraft design that could be controlled by a pilot. Gliders had flown and models had been launched, but none were controlled by anything other than the wind. The first airplane that could be controlled— up, down, side to side, and when landing—would make history.

Several of the Wright brothers' models failed. In 1903, however, they came up with a new design that they thought might work. Orville and Wilbur traveled with it to Kitty Hawk, North Carolina. The soft sands on the beach there, blasted by steady winds, made it the ideal site.

December 17, 1903, was biting cold. The brothers were tired and wanted to get home for Christmas, so they decided to give

their Wright *Flyer* a final test. Orville climbed into the pilot's seat (the brothers took turns taking test flights). With the help of a local crew, Orville aimed the *Flyer* into the wind and gunned the engine.

Slowly, shakily—but steadily—the *Flyer* soared, and 120 feet (37 m) later, it landed softly. It was the first controlled airplane flight in history. The brothers took turns making other flights that day, a total of four, the longest of which was more than 800 feet (244 m).

Word of their success spread quickly. The brothers became world famous. Their invention and hard work paved the way for the aerial world we live in today.

There are dozens of great books about these important inventors. Also, check out these Web sites: www.first-to-fly.com, which includes a museum of aviation; and www.nasm.si.edu, the National Air and Space Museum site.

Early Flight Firsts

Just about every flight taken in the early years of airplanes brought about some sort of first. Here are some of the most interesting:

First passenger: Charles Furnas, May 14, 1908, in a plane piloted by Wilbur Wright

First air show: August 1909, near Reims, France

First licensed pilot: The Aero Club of America gave its first official pilot's license to Glenn Curtiss on June 8, 1911.

First female pilot: On March 8, 1910, Baroness de Laroche of France earned the world's first official pilot's license given to a woman. On August 11, 1911, the Aero Club of America licensed Harriet Quimby, America's first female pilot.

Not Flying—Falling!

In 1797, André-Jacques Garnerin made the first recorded parachute jump. Near Paris, France, he dropped out of a balloon basket with a parachute-like silk cloth over his head. He landed safely. In 1912, Albert Perry made the first parachute jump from a plane flying over St. Louis. A year later, Georgia Broadwick was the first woman to parachute from a plane.

First night flights: (World) Emil Aubrun in Argentina on March 10, 1910. (U.S.) Walter Brookins, April 18, 1910, near Montgomery, Alabama. In 1916, Ruth Law became the first woman to fly at night, piloting a plane from Chicago, Illinois, to Hornell, New York.

First flight across English Channel: July 25, 1909, by famed aviator Louis Blériot; his flight took 37 minutes.

First takeoff from a ship: November 14, 1910, by Eugene Burton off the Navy cruiser *Birmingham,* off the coast of Virginia

First takeoff and landing on water: Glenn Curtiss demonstrated that his "hydroaeroplane" could really work (and not sink!) on January 26, 1911.

First large group of people: On March 23, 1911, French pilot Louis Breguet carried 11 people three miles (4.8 km) in a very large airplane he designed himself. It was the first time more than two people had flown at one time.

First airmail service: The first flight to carry mail was on February 18, 1911, on the first-ever nonstop flight from Paris to London by Pierre Prier. Shortly after, British pilots started the first regular airmail service. The first letters sent via regular airmail were addressed to Britain's King George V.

Amazing Amelia

Amelia Earhart was the first woman to fly across the Atlantic Ocean by herself. But that was not all she did first in the sky. Amelia was among the most famous aviators in history. Here are some of her most famous firsts:

Londonderry, Ireland, covering more than 2,000 miles (3,218 km) in just under 15 hours.

❋ First transcontinental nonstop flight by a woman: Leaving from Los Angeles, California, on August 24, 1932, Earhart flew without a break for 19 hours, landing in Newark, New Jersey.

❋ First woman to fly across the Atlantic: June 18, 1928. Flying with pilot Bill Stultz and navigator Slim Gordon, Earhart took 20 hours and 40 minutes to go from Newfoundland, Canada, to Wales in Great Britain.

❋ First woman to fly solo across the Atlantic: July 20–21, 1932. She flew from Newfoundland, Canada, to

❋ First Hawaii-mainland solo flight by anyone: January 1935. Earhart took about 18 hours to fly from Honolulu to Oakland, California, over nothing but water.

❋ On July 2, 1937, she and navigator Fred Noonan disappeared over the Pacific Ocean while Earhart was trying to become the first woman to fly around the world!

Lucky Lindy

Charles Lindbergh stunned the world in 1927 when he flew his plane, The Spirit of St. Louis, *across the Atlantic Ocean. Flying solo, he left on May 20 and took 33 hours, 32 minutes to fly from Long Island, New York, to a field near Paris, France. So excited were his well-wishers that they nearly tore "Lucky Lindy" and his plane apart. Here are more facts about this famous first flight:*

✳ Lindbergh could not see out of the front windows of his airplane. He needed so much fuel to make the Atlantic crossing that he had put another gas tank on the plane that blocked his forward visibility.

✳ Lindbergh's greatest challenge was staying awake for the transatlantic journey. He sang and talked to himself to keep from sleeping.

✳ On takeoff, his plane was so heavy that he nearly collided with electric power lines just beyond the runway.

✳ Lindbergh packed four sandwiches and two canteens of water to eat and drink during the flight.

✳ Nearing the coast of Ireland, he flew low over a fishing boat and tried to yell down at a fisherman to get directions to the coastline. Not surprisingly, the man couldn't hear him!

✳ On his approach to the landing zone, the field was so crowded with people that he could barely find a place for his airplane!

✳ To return to the U.S., Lindbergh boarded the USS *Memphis* warship, sent by President Calvin Coolidge to pick up America's newest hero, the "Lone Eagle."

✳ Upon his return to the U.S., he received the largest ticker-tape parade ever given through New York City's Wall Street district.

✳ Lindbergh's airplane can be seen at the National Air and Space Museum. It has a wingspan of 46 feet (14 m).

Around the

It's a big world, and when people suddenly found themselves above it in aircraft, they wanted to go around it, too. Here are some firsts in circumnavigation (flying around something—in this case, the world):

First solo: Wiley Post flew more than 15,000 miles (24,000 km) from July 15 to July 22, 1933. After leaving from New York City, he stopped ten times to refuel. The year before, Post had flown around the world, but that flight was made with a copilot.

First without landing: The ability to refuel planes in flight led to this record first. On February 26, 1949, a U.S. Army Air Corps B-50 Superfortress took off from Fort Worth, Texas. It didn't land again for more than 94 hours and 23,500 miles (37,800 km). While in the air, the B-50 was refueled four times!

First group of jets: In 1957, three U.S. Air Force B-52 jets flew together nonstop around the world. The planes were refueled in midair by special tanker jets.

First commercial flight: In 1941, in a Pan American Airways Pacific Clipper airplane, Captain Richard Ford and his crew took 209 hours over the course of a month to fly 31,500 miles (50,700 km). They left from San Francisco and stopped 13 times before completing the circle (well, almost) in New York City. In 1947, Pan Am started the first scheduled flights for

World in 80 Ways

passengers around the world. The 13-stop, 101-hour flight cost $1,700. Passengers could stay at each stop for a day or so.

First without refueling: An amazing feat of engineering combined with some serious human endurance power in 1986. Designer/pilot Richard Rutan and copilot Jeana Yeager flew entirely around the world without landing or refueling. Their special plane, called *Voyager*, was pretty much a flying gas tank. The two aviators spent nine days in the cockpit, taking turns sleeping and flying this unique craft.

First in a balloon: Many people tried to fly around the world in a balloon, but technical problems or weather always stopped them. Finally, in 2002, Steve Fossett piloted the 140-foot (43-m) *Spirit of Freedom* to and from Australia in 16 days. Fossett also holds balloon firsts for crossing four different continents and the Pacific Ocean.

POLE

Over the Poles

The mysterious ice caps at the North and South Poles were just beginning to be explored in the early 20th century. Some explorers recognized that flying over the poles in an airplane would be the best and safest way to survey these remote areas. Admiral Richard Byrd led the way, first flying over the North Pole in 1926 and later, the South Pole in 1929.

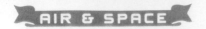
Unusual Air Firsts

You've heard of the Wright brothers and Amelia Earhart . . . maybe even about the Montgolfiers. But here are some odd "air firsts" that you might not have heard of (or even thought about!):

First in-flight meal: June 1914: Served aboard the German zeppelin airship *Ilia Mouriametz*. Passengers enjoyed turkey and vegetables.

First in-flight movie: On a 1925 flight across Europe, Imperial Airways finally found something to entertain passengers— they showed newsreels (short documentaries). In 1961, TWA became the first airline to show movies on all of their long flights.

First in-flight magazine: At last, something to put in the seat pocket! *Clipper* magazine was first published in 1947 by Pan American Airlines.

MY FIRST...

I took my first airplane ride when I was _____ years old. We flew from _____

to _____.

We were going to see _____.

I thought it was _____.

First wrong-way Atlantic crossing: In 1929, pilot Douglas Corrigan told airport officials in New York he was flying to California. He took off and 29 hours later...landed in Ireland! He claimed his compass had malfunctioned, and "Wrong Way" Corrigan became an international hero for "accidentally" crossing the Atlantic Ocean solo.

First airplane loop-the-loop: This is a tricky maneuver in which a pilot flies in a complete circle, turning upside down at the top before once again flying in the same direction. Lincoln Beachley did it first, above San Diego, California, on November 18, 1913.

First way to sleep on an airplane: American Airways put in special seats that unfolded into cots in 1933.

First flight attendant: Heinrich Kubis served drinks on a zeppelin in Germany in 1912.

First female flight attendant: Ellen Church joined Boeing Air Transport in May 1930. Her first flight was from San Francisco, California, to Cheyenne, Wyoming.

First frequent-flyer program: American Airlines created the AAdvantage Program in 1981. Passengers earned "miles" for flying on American Airlines. Those miles earned free or discounted flights. Most airlines now offer similar programs.

Going Really Fast

Once people figured out how to fly (and land, of course), the next step was easy: fly faster. From the Wright brothers to today, going faster and faster in the air has been a primary goal. The biggest news in aircraft speed came with the invention of the jet engine.

200 Miles (320 km) Per Hour

Early airplanes were not very fast. You could probably ride your bike as fast as the Wright brothers' plane. Even early biplanes didn't go much faster than your family car on the highway. So being the first to reach 200 miles (322 km) per hour was big! In 1922, Lester Maitland flew his propeller plane 216 miles (348 km) per hour.

Here Come the Jets

Jet aircraft use powerful engines to reach very high speeds. The first jet flight was on August 27, 1940, by the Italian-made CC2. The first American jet airplane, the XP-59, was flown by Robert Stanley in California at a speed of more than 400 miles (644 km) per hour.

Going Up and Down

Airplanes were going very, very fast, but only in one direction at a time. Meanwhile, many people were looking at another kind of aircraft—the helicopter.

Leonardo da Vinci drew a device like a helicopter in 1483. His device had a rotating wing above the passenger seat, but it was never built. In the centuries that followed, many engineers and scientists advanced helicopter designs one idea at a time.

Sir George Cayley, Paul Cornu, Juan de la Cierva, and Americans

Mach 1

The greatest barrier in speed was one no one could see: the sound barrier. Sound travels in waves through the air at about 750 miles (1,207 km) per hour. Engineers worried that an aircraft going that fast would hit an invisible "wall." Finally, the wall fell. On October 14, 1947, Chuck Yeager, an Air Force test pilot, flew his Bell X-1 rocket plane to a speed of Mach ("mock") 1.06. Mach 1 is the name for the sound barrier—which Yeager had broken.

Concorde

Passenger jets cruise along below the speed of sound, except for one famous airplane. In 1969, the Concorde became the first passenger jet to exceed Mach 1. Its top speed was more than 1,342 miles (2,160 km) per hour. However, it was very expensive to operate. The last Concorde flight was in 2003.

Fastest Piloted Flight Ever

On October 3, 1967, Major William Knight set the world speed record for an airplane when he flew the experimental X-15 rocket plane more than 4,500 miles (7,242 km) per hour.

Emile and Henry Berliner all built aircraft that used rotating blades. None of them, however, built a model that could successfully take off vertically (straight up) and then fly forward and backward while safely carrying a pilot.

In 1939, Igor Sikorsky's VS-300 model became the first "true" helicopter. The Russian-born engineer refined it many times and became the leader in helicopter innovations. Helicopters play an important role in the world of flight today. Sikorsky's is considered the first, but the helicopter was really the result of many people's ideas.

First into Space

Rocket Power!

Airplanes and other aircraft let human beings leave the ground for the first time. The invention of rocket power meant that they could leave the planet altogether. Beginning in 1914, American scientist Robert Goddard perfected many types of rockets. (He holds more than 200 patents!) He flew the first rocket powered by liquid fuel on March 16, 1926.

A few decades later, scientists used rocket power to send human beings (and other things, see page 32) into outer space for the first time. Here's a look at some of the brave pioneers of space:

First Satellite

On October 4, 1957, the Soviet Union (USSR*) sent the first object from Earth into outer space. The satellite, called *Sputnik I*, ignited the "space race." The USSR and the United States would battle for the next 30 years, reaching farther and farther out from our "little blue marble." The first American satellite was called *Explorer 1* and was launched in January 1958.

*Beginning in 1989, the USSR, which stood for Union of Soviet Socialist Republics, split up into Russia, the Ukraine, Belarus, and many other smaller countries.

First Man

Soviet Army Major Yuri Gagarin flew around Earth in the spacecraft *Vostok 1* on April 12, 1961.

First U.S. Man

Astronaut Alan Shepard, Jr., rocketed into space on May 5, 1961. John Glenn, Jr., became the first American to orbit Earth in 1962.

First Woman

Soviet cosmonaut Valentina Tereshkova circled Earth 48 times in June 1963. (The first American woman astronaut did not travel to space until June 18, 1983, when Sally Ride flew aboard the space shuttle *Challenger*.)

First Space Walk

Space suits allowed astronauts to survive the airless, freezing cold of space. On March 18, 1965, cosmonaut Alexei Leonov, tied to his craft by a special cord, became the first person to float free in space, which he did for 12 amazing minutes.

First Space Station

Flying to and from space was fine, but what about a longer stay? That became possible in 1971 with the launch of the *Salyut* space station by the USSR. The first U.S. space station was *Skylab 1*, launched in 1973.

The Moon

Pretty much anything to do with humans and the Moon was a first. Here are some of the most interesting firsts, followed by a longer description of perhaps the single most famous first in this whole book!

First Earth craft to land on the Moon: USSR's *Luna 2* probe smacked into the surface on September 12, 1959.

First orbital pictures taken of the Moon: USSR's *Luna 3* in October 1959

First close-up pictures of the Moon: Taken by space probe *Ranger 7*, July 31, 1964

First U.S. craft to orbit the Moon: *Lunar Orbiter 1*, 1966

First orbit of the Moon by humans: Frank Borman, James Lovell, and William Anders spun around the Moon ten times

Planetary Firsts

With the Moon "conquered," humans set their sights on other planets. Although no person has yet visited another planet, various machines, probes, and craft have either circled or landed on all eight of our fellow planets. Here's when they were (or will be) visited first:

Mercury: 1974	Jupiter: 1973	Neptune: 1977
Venus: 1970	Saturn: 1974	Pluto: Planned
Mars: 1965	Uranus: 1977	for 2015

in *Apollo 8* in 1968. They were the first humans to see the far side of the Moon from space.

First meal on the Moon: While in their landing craft, Neil Armstrong and Edwin "Buzz" Aldrin (see below) ate bacon squares, sugar cookies, and peaches.

First craft to drive on the Moon: The Lunar Rover was brought by *Apollo 15* in 1971. Astronauts drove it around the Moon's surface.

First golfer on the Moon: In 1971, Alan Shepard smacked a golf ball with a digging tool while taking a break from his work exploring the Moon.

First Humans on the Moon!

In 1968, *Apollo 8* became the first manned craft to orbit the Moon. But that was just the beginning. A little more than a year later, on July 20, 1969, one of the most momentous events in human history occurred: Flying in *Apollo 11*, humans landed on and walked on the surface of the Moon!

It may be hard to understand just how big a deal this was. The scientists at the time were using about as much computing power as contained in a handful of your school's computers. They didn't know what would happen when the astronauts stepped out. Would they sink into the surface? Would the atmosphere inside their capsule, designed to help them breathe, ignite when they opened the door?

An estimated 1 billion people watched live on television as Neil Armstrong took the final step off the ladder onto the lunar surface. His footsteps were the first mark human beings had ever made on another celestial body. Joined by fellow astronaut Edwin Aldrin, Armstrong became perhaps the most famous first in history.

Shuttle Firsts

In 1981, the United States debuted a stunning new way to explore outer space: the space shuttle. Launched while strapped to two huge rockets, the shuttle was the first craft that could fly into space, orbit Earth, and then land back on Earth like an airplane. Being able to reuse a spacecraft meant that many more flights could be made. This chart lists some of the more interesting and historic firsts that have happened on shuttle flights.

YEAR	FIRST	SHUTTLE
1981	Shuttle flight	Columbia
1981	Crew: John Young and Robert Crippen	Columbia
1982	Placing satellites in orbit from within shuttle	Columbia
1983	Space walk from shuttle	Challenger
1983	American woman in space	Challenger
1983	Nighttime launch and landing	Challenger
1983	Astronaut from European Space Agency: West German Ulf Merbold	Columbia
1984	Space walk not attached to spacecraft	Challenger

Before the First?

John Young and Robert Crippen took the space shuttle into space for the first time. But two other astronauts, Joe Engle and Richard Truly, played a big role. They were the first to fly the shuttle in the lower atmosphere and to practice landing it. Though they never made it into space, they were the first people at the controls of the shuttle.

YEAR	FIRST	SHUTTLE
1985	U.S. senator in space: Jake Garn of Utah	Discovery
1985	Animals on the shuttle: 2 monkeys, 24 mice	Challenger
1992	Married couple as crew members: Mark Lee and Jan Davis	Endeavour
1995	Female pilot: Eileen Collins	Discovery
1995	Docking linkup with space station (Mir)	Atlantis
1998	Person over 65 years old: Senator John Glenn	Discovery
1999	Female commander: Eileen Collins	Columbia

World of Space

Though only a handful of countries have sent rockets into outer space, no one nation can truly claim "ownership" of the heavens. As the space programs in the United States, Russia, and Europe have grown over the years, more and more people from around the world have become the first from their countries to fly into space. Here is a sampling of first space travelers from a variety of countries:

COUNTRY	ASTRONAUT	YEAR
Australia	Andy Thomas	1996
Canada	Marc Garneau	1984
Cuba	Arnaldo Tamayo-Mendez	1980
France	Jean-Loup Chrétien	1982
Germany*	Ulf Merbold	1983
Great Britain	Helen Sharman	1991
India	Rakesh Sharma	1984
Mexico	Rodolfo Neri Vela	1985
Mongolia	Jugderdemidiyn Gurragcha	1981
Netherlands	Lodewijk van den Berg	1985
Poland	Miroslaw Hermaszewski	1978
Saudi Arabia	Sultan Salman Abdel-aziz Al-Saud	1985
Vietnam	Pham Tuan	1980

* West Germany; East German Sigmund Jahn flew in 1978

More Pioneers

➲ In 1983, Guion Bluford, Jr., became the first African American in space. He flew aboard the space shuttle *Challenger*. Dr. Mae Jemison was the first African-American woman, when working on the *Endeavour* in 1992.

➲ Ellen Ochoa was the first Hispanic American, when she took off on *Discovery* in 1993. She took part in three other shuttle flights.

first-rate Of the highest quality and importance. It can also mean "very well," as in "everything is just first-rate."

THE FIRST...

Planet from the Sun 1

Counting out from the Sun, Mercury is the first planet in the solar system. Here are five cool things about the very hot first planet:

1 To begin with, Mercury is anything but cool. Being so close to the Sun, it is both extremely hot and cold, with surface temperatures ranging from $-328°F$ ($-200°C$) to $752°F$ ($400°C$)!

2 Mercury is named for the Roman god of travel; he was also the messenger of the gods.

3 The Sumerians of 3000 BCE were the first people to note the appearance of Mercury in their sky.

4 Most of the material that makes up the planet Mercury is solid iron.

5 On Mercury, an 80-pound (36.3-kg) kid would weigh just 30.4 pounds (13.7 kg)!

More Space Firsts

We have enough . . . space (sorry about that) for a few more firsts that are out of this world:

☞ *Pioneer 10* was the first object made by humans to leave the solar system. The probe whizzed past the path of Pluto in 1983.

☞ The first photo from the giant Hubble Space Telescope, launched on April 24, 1990, was beamed back on May 20 of that year. It showed a distant star cluster in the constellation Carina.

☞ Animals actually went into space long before the first human ever hopped on board a rocket ship. Here are the first animals sent into space:

● Laika, a dog, became the first Earth creature sent into space in 1957 when she traveled on a USSR rocket. Sadly, she did not survive the journey.

● A monkey named Sam flew just below space orbit in a Mercury capsule in 1959. A chimpanzee named Enos was the first primate to make it into orbit in 1961.

● In the 1970s, U.S. and Soviet space flights carried rats, newts, fruit flies, and green tree frogs (though not all at the same time . . .).

☞ Until 1986, all space travelers were highly trained scientists, pilots, engineers, doctors, or other specialists. Then New Hampshire teacher Christa McAuliffe was chosen to represent millions, actually billions, of "regular" people as the first teacher in space. Sadly, a midair accident caused *Challenger* to explode, killing McAuliffe and the other six members of her crew.

☞ In 2001, American businessman Dennis Tito became the first tourist in space. He paid the Russian space agency more than $20 million. After undergoing months of training, Tito blasted off and spent five days in space aboard a Soyuz spacecraft that was delivering parts to the International Space Station.

Other Ways to Fly

Solar-Powered Flight

The Sun is the biggest power source near Earth. Not until December 3, 1979, however, did someone come up with a way of harnessing that power to fly. Pilot Janice Brown flew the *Solar Challenger* airplane for more than three miles (4.8 km) in Arizona. The aluminum and plastic plane was covered with solar panels that converted the Sun's rays directly into power to fly the plane.

Human-Powered Flight

In 1977, an engineer named Paul McReady created the *Gossamer Condor,* an ultralight craft covered with plastic sheeting. Inside, he put a cyclist named Bryan Allen, who pedaled to supply the plane's power. On August 23, 1977, Allen flew the plane for more than three miles (4.8 km), becoming the first human to "fly" under his own power.

SAY IT FIRST...

first class Something that is of the highest quality. The phrase is also used to describe the most expensive and most comfortable section of a passenger plane. It is usually located at the very front of the aircraft.

Mars Firsts

In 2004, the world watched in wonder as two specially designed unmanned spacecraft landed on the surface of Mars. Earth's nearest planetary neighbor has provided many exciting firsts:

First "flyby" of Mars: The *Mariner 4* satellite zoomed by Mars on July 14 and 15, 1965. It sent back the first photos of the planet taken from close range (as opposed to being taken with telescopes). *Mariner 4* did not orbit Mars, however.

First orbit of Mars: The *Mariner 9* satellite was the first Earth spacecraft ever to orbit another planet. It went around Mars twice a day for a year beginning in June 1971.

First craft to land on Mars: The *Mars 3* module landed in December 1971, but was damaged on impact and transmitted a signal for only a few seconds.

First craft to land successfully on Mars: *Viking 1* and *Viking 2* landed safely on Mars in 1976. They were not mobile, but stayed in one spot and sent back the first close-up photos and video of the surface of Mars.

First craft to drive on Mars: On July 5, 1997, after a bumpy landing, the Mars rover *Sojourner* rolled away from its landing site. Computers from Earth directed its movements and transmitted the first photos of the Martian surface back to Earth. In 2004, two more rovers, *Opportunity* and *Spirit,* also delivered close-up pictures of the Martian surface for us to marvel.

First human to land on Mars: Let us know when you get there!

CHAPTER 2

Entertainment

You enjoy entertainment of all sorts. In this chapter, read about firsts in movies, television, books, music, comic books, and more.

Action! Birth of the Movies

Photography has been around since the 1820s (see page 274), but it took a while longer before people figured out how to make pictures move! Movies (or motion pictures) work by stringing together individual pictures of action. Shown in sequence at a rapid rate, they create the illusion of motion on the flat surface of a screen.

The first photographer to try this successfully was Eadweard Muybridge. In 1872, he took a series of photos of a horse running. Projecting them rapidly one after another created the illusion that the horse was really moving. But Muybridge used individual cameras taking one frame at a time. They were tripped by the horse's hooves as it ran by.

In 1882, French inventor Etienne-Jules Marey first made a machine that took 12 pictures in one second. In 1885, Louis Le Prince created a camera that took even more photos for a longer period of time. Sadly, he died soon after and could not expand on his ideas.

Others did, however, and on December 28, 1895, Auguste and Louis Lumière showed a motion picture on a machine they called a "cinématographe" (from which we get the word *cinema*, used to describe both the movies and the place where they are shown). Most movie historians call this event the real birth of "the movies."

Here Comes Edison

The famous inventor Thomas Edison played a key role in making the idea of watching movies popular. His employee William Dickson created a film strip that could be viewed on a machine by one person at a time. Surprisingly, Edison did not at first think that a lot of people would sit in one place long enough to watch a longer film.

He soon changed his mind, however, and helped create the Vitascope machine to flash movies onto a screen for many people to watch. The first time Americans paid to sit in a dark theater to watch a film came on April 23, 1896, in New York. They watched some women dancing and then waves crashing on a beach.

Other Early Film Firsts

Movie studio: Opened in 1893 in West Orange, New Jersey

Movie theater: At 1155 Broadway in New York City, in 1894 to show film strips only

Edited film: Most films in these early days were shot with one camera in sequence. The editing process so familiar to today's audiences was not a part of the first movies. Edwin Porter changed that in his *Life of an American Fireman* in 1902, when he was the first to edit a film to show different points of view.

ACTION!

Movie stars: Most early movie stars were not named in the film's credits. Bronco Billy Anderson broke that mold when he starred in Westerns from 1908 to 1915 and was the first male American "movie star." In 1910, Florence Lawrence was the first female actress to get credit and, with it, piles of public attention.

Movie Mania

With the invention of movie cameras and projectors, artists found a new way to tell stories. Over the first few years of moviemaking, they created most of the types of movies we are familiar with today. Here are the first examples of different types of films:

First Western: *Kit Carson*, 1903. (The famous film *The Great Train Robbery* came out four months later. Its popularity established Westerns as an important and popular type of movie.)

First feature film: (longer than one hour) *The Story of the Kelly Gang*, made in Australia in 1906

First science fiction: *A Trip to the Moon*, 1902

First comedy: A short untitled film about a boy playing tricks on people with a garden hose, 1895

First horror: *Dr. Jekyll and Mr. Hyde*, 1908

First musical: *The Jazz Singer*, 1927. (Although other films had music in them, this was the first to combine it with the storyline of the movie.) The first color musical was 1939's *The Wizard of Oz*. That movie (as you probably know) opens in black-and-white. When Dorothy gets to Oz, the film changes to bright color.

First documentary: *Nanook of the North*, 1922

In Color . . . and Sound!

Today moviegoers are used to vibrant colors and nearly deafening sound. Early filmgoers, however, watched in black-and-white and heard nothing, except perhaps a piano player. It was time to brighten up the movies!

First color film: In 1906, Englishman George Smith experimented with the first color film, taking pictures of his children playing in their yard. Though some color films were made and shown to the public, using Smith's technique, it was very expensive. The first color film that was both successful and affordable was *Flowers and Trees (A Silly Symphony)*, produced by Walt Disney in 1932. Yes, *that* Disney!

First talkies!: Thomas Edison, inventor of both the phonograph and an early type of motion picture, was key to adding sound to the movies. In 1895, he created the Kinetophone, which merged a wax cylinder sound recording with a film strip. In 1906, Eugène Lauste was the first to merge sound and picture on the same piece of film. In 1922, Lee de Forest's Phonofilm process proved to be the best solution yet. It was used to make the 1927 movie *The Jazz Singer*, which is considered the first "talking" film. Earlier sound movies used music, not speech.

First Drive-In Theater

It opened in 1933 in Camden, New Jersey. People never had to leave their cars when they went out to the movies . . . except to get popcorn, of course.

Before Nemo

Animation is basically what the movies are: A series of pictures, in this case drawings, that are shown rapidly to create the illusion of motion. Here are some key firsts in the history of animated film:

First animated cartoon: In 1906, artist James Blackton drew more than 8,000 pictures that he combined into *Humorous Phases of Funny Faces.*

First animated cartoon character: Gertie the Trained Dinosaur, 1910, by Winsor McCay

First color cartoon: *The Debut of Thomas Kat*, 1916

First sound cartoon: *Steamboat Willie* (1928) by Walt Disney; also the first appearance of Mickey Mouse.

First full-length cartoon movie: Disney's *Snow White and the Seven Dwarfs* in 1937.

First computer-animated film: The first feature made on computers was *Toy Story*, released in 1995.

3-D Movies

Have you ever seen a 3-D movie? They're pretty cool. A unique filming process lets someone wearing special glasses see the actors "coming out" of the screen. The "3-D" stands for "three-dimensional." The first 3-D movie was made in 1922, called *The Power of Love.*

Many 3-D films were made in the 1950s when movie studios were trying to lure people back to the movies after the invention of TV.

first run This term describes the first time a movie is released to theaters for the public to see.

Their First Movie

Some of your favorite movie stars didn't start out in big, blockbuster films. Here are the names and release dates of the first on-screen appearances by some of today's biggest stars:

STAR	MOVIE	YEAR
Amanda Bynes	*Big Fat Liar*	2002
Jim Carrey	*All in Good Taste*	1983
Hilary Duff	*Human Nature*	2001
Frankie Muniz	*Little Man*	1999
Mary-Kate and Ashley Olsen	*The Little Rascals*	1994
Tobey Maguire	*The Wizard*	1989
Mike Myers	*Wayne's World*	1992
Adam Sandler	*Going Overboard*	1989

Oscar Firsts

The Academy Awards were first given out in 1929. The first Best Picture was Wings, *a silent movie about World War I flying aces. Emil Jannings was the first Best Actor and Janet Gaynor was the first Best Actress.* The Jazz Singer *received a special award for "pioneering . . . talking pictures."*

No one really knows who first started calling the gold Academy Award statue the "Oscar," but the term has been in regular use since the mid-1930s. Here are some fun Oscar firsts:

The first child actor to win an Oscar was Shirley Temple, who was six when she was given an honorary Oscar in 1934.

It Happened One Night (1934) was the first movie to win all five of the major Oscars (Best Picture, Actor, Actress, Director, and Screenplay).

Hattie McDaniel's Best Supporting Actress award in 1939 (for *Gone with the Wind*) was the first won by an African American. Sidney Poitier's 1963 performance in *Lilies of the Field* made him the first African-American Best Actor winner.

In 1941, Orson Welles became the first person to be nominated in the same year for Best Producer, Director, Actor, and Screenwriter for *Citizen Kane*.

The Oscar ceremony was first televised in 1953.

The first child actor to win a non-honorary Oscar was Tatum O'Neal, who was ten when she was named Best Supporting Actress for *Paper Moon* in 1974.

The first animated movie ever nominated for Best Picture was *Beauty and the Beast* in 1992.

The first non–American-made film to win Best Picture was *Hamlet* in 1948.

A major new category was added to the Oscars in 2002—Best Animated Picture. *Shrek* was the first winner.

Money, Money, Money

One of the ways that the movie industry ranks its films is by what is called "box office gross." That doesn't mean gross like yucky, but gross as in "total." Here are some historic firsts in the battle of box office grosses (based on U.S. ticket sales):

The first movie to earn **$100 million** was the shark-attack drama *Jaws*, released in 1975. People might have been afraid to go in the water, but not into the movie theaters. *Jaws* was also the first movie to reach the **$200 million** mark! Another watery movie made history in 1997. After becoming the first movie with **$500 million** in American sales, *Titanic* was also the first movie to go over **$1 billion** (with a B!) in world ticket sales. In 1994, *Titanic's* director, James Cameron, made the first movie to *cost* more than $100 million—*True Lies*, starring Arnold Schwarzenegger.

MY FIRST...

The first movie I saw in a theater was _____
_____.

I was _____ years old.
The first book I read all by myself was _____
_____.

The first TV show I remember watching regularly was _____
_____.

Click! TV Turns On

Television, that thing you think you couldn't do without, is less than 100 years old. Many inventors had a hand in its development. Here are some of the notable first steps:

■→ In 1884, Germany's Paul Nipkow had the idea of breaking up a picture into electronic bits that could be transmitted. This idea is the basis for modern television.

■→ Karl Braun of Germany invented the cathode-ray tube in 1897; this would later become the essential part of every television system.

■→ Scotsman Alan Swinton wrote a 1907 article that described how to send images and sound electronically using cathode-ray tubes, which is what the first real TVs ended up using.

■→ J. L. Baird and Charles Jenkins each transmitted fuzzy-looking pictures by wire in 1926.

■→ In 1929, Russian Vladimir Zworykin patented a system that used cathode rays to transmit electronic pictures.

■→ Philo T. Farnsworth came along in 1930 to finally perfect the cathode-ray tube TV transmission method. Farnsworth's work is considered the "invention" of TV, but he was building on the work of many scientists who had come before him.

Early TV Firsts

■→ TV station WGY in New York City broadcast the first regular TV signals in 1928.

■→ In 1925, William Taynton was working near scientist

J. L. Baird's office. The 15-year-old boy became the first person ever to be on television when Baird used Taynton as a test subject for his first transmission of a live picture.

➤➤ The first scheduled TV program was on July 21, 1931. It featured music, speeches, and comedians.

➤➤ In Great Britain, the BBC (British Broadcasting Corporation) started regular broadcasts in 1932.

➤➤ The first broadcast of a live major league baseball game came on August 26, 1939, between the Cincinnati Reds and the Brooklyn Dodgers.

➤➤ The first TV commercial was shown in 1941. It was for Bulova Watch Co. and cost Bulova nine dollars!

In Color!

All early television was in black-and-white. In 1904, a German system for color TV was patented, but it didn't work well. The first successful public showing of color television came on January 9, 1941, by scientists at Bell Labs under contract to CBS. By 1951, people could buy very expensive color TV sets and watch some programs in color. But the quality of the sets wasn't very high and the experiment failed.

Production stopped while companies focused their energy on the Korean War (1951–53). In 1954, RCA began selling the first affordable color TV sets to the public. In 1961, Walt Disney's *World of Color* TV show debuted and inspired millions to purchase color sets. In 1966, NBC became the first network to show almost all of its programming in color.

Hot New Shows!

All of your favorite TV shows had to start somewhere. Here is a list of when people watched the first episodes of some famous kids' or family TV shows from past and present:

YEAR	SHOW
1967	Mister Rogers' Neighborhood
1969	The Brady Bunch
1969	Sesame Street
1969	Scooby-Doo, Where Are You?
1971	The Electric Company
1972	Fat Albert and the Cosby Kids
1973	SuperFriends
1974	Little House on the Prairie
1984	Transformers
1989	The Simpsons
1991	Rugrats
1994	Sister, Sister
1998	Pokémon (U.S. debut)
1998	Powerpuff Girls
1998	Yu-Gi-Oh
1999	Spongebob Squarepants
1999	Batman Beyond
2000	Jackie Chan Adventures

Gearing Up

You can't watch TV without a lot of snazzy electronic gear. But when was that gear available for the first time?

First television set used in public: On
August 20, 1930, at 98 Riverside Drive in New York City, an experimental television set received 30 minutes of programming. It was the first time a TV had been used in a private home.

First video tape recorder: Invented in 1951 by a
team led by engineer Charles Ginsburg, this reel-to-reel machine was used to save copies of TV shows.

First VCR: The first videocassette recorder was not the
now-familiar VHS (Video Home System) format, but a smaller size called a Betamax. It was first sold in America in 1975. The first VHS VCRs were sold in 1976. They soon overtook Betamax and became the standard video format.

First satellite dish: The first personal satellite dish
was invented in 1976 by Taylor Howard to capture more TV signals for the home.

First DVD: In 1995, several large electronics
companies jointly released the first DVDs (digital video discs). They saw what had happened to VCRs and decided to manufacture just one format.

First TV remote control: Made in
1956 by Robert Adler

TV Shows

American TV is filled with a wide variety of programming. (No, it's true! Even if all you watch is cartoons or sports!) Most of today's shows have their roots in early television. Here is when America saw the debut of some of these types of shows:

First drama series: Kraft Television Theater, 1947

First Western series: Hopalong Cassidy, 1948

First sitcom: The Goldbergs, 1949

First soap opera: These Are My Children, 1949

First animated cartoon: Crusader Rabbit, 1949

First cartoon in prime time: The Flintstones, 1960

First series regularly broadcast in color:
Bonanza, beginning in 1959

First TV Dinner

The first TV dinners were created by the Swanson Company in 1953. They included an entire meal, cooked at one time. The idea was that folks could make a quick dinner and eat it while watching TV. The first dinners offered turkey, potatoes, and vegetables on an aluminum tray.

Cable Firsts

For most of television's lifetime, the signals needed to put pictures in your set zipped through the air. The signals, still sent that way, are free to anyone with an antenna.

In 1948, a Pennsylvania TV store owner named John Walson changed TV forever. He connected his customers' sets via a cable to a large antenna. That helped them receive many more channels than they had previously had. It was called Community Antenna TV (CATV) and later "cable TV." Eventually, the idea of bringing programming via cables (and later satellites) boomed. People did not seem to mind paying for the ability to receive many, many more programs than were available on "free TV." In 1999, for the first time, more people were watching cable TV than were watching the four major non-cable networks. Here are some firsts from the world of cable TV:

First CATV systems: Pennsylvania and Oregon, 1948

First sporting event broadcast on cable: Floyd Patterson–Ingemar Johannson boxing match, 1961

First original production for cable television: The 1973 Pennsylvania Polka Festival

First national pay-cable network: Home Box Office (HBO), 1972

First use of satellite in a cable system: 1973

First appearance of some cable networks:

ESPN	1979	BET	1980	MTV	1981
C-SPAN	1979	USA	1980	Weather Channel	1982
Nickelodeon*	1979	CNN	1980	Discovery	1985

* Nick debuted as a channel called Pinwheel. It became Nickelodeon in 1981.

Books Are Born

People have been writing for thousands of years. Neanderthals made pictures on cave walls, but it's hard to carry a cave around with you in your backpack. Ancient Egyptians used a type of paper called papyrus to record events, which was certainly more portable. In Europe, medieval monks carefully copied texts one at a time by hand, binding them together in book form. Chinese scrolls show illustrations and writing, printed from wood blocks, as early as 868 CE.

The key to the first modern "book," however, was to find a way to recreate the same text without hand copying it character by character. In the ninth century, Chinese artists created a kind of movable type; that is, bits of wood that could be combined to form words and sentences. In Europe, however, Johannes Gutenberg of Germany was the first to print a complete book using type. He chose the Bible, and its first edition was issued in 1451. It was the first book that could be reprinted over and over exactly the same way.

SAY IT FIRST...

first edition
A term from publishing that refers to the first version of a book. Some first editions of books by famous or popular authors can be very valuable. First editions of very old books are prized by collectors and can be worth a large amount of money. Check to see if you have the first edition of this book by looking on the copyright page (that's on page 2!). About three-quarters of the way down the page, look for a list of little numbers starting with 10 and counting down. If the final number in the list is 1, you have a first edition. Save this book!

Stacking Books

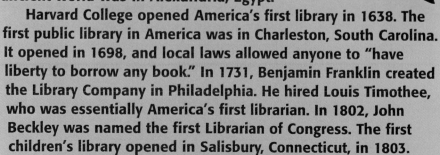

One place to find books, of course, is in a library. Libraries, too, have been around for many centuries. One of the largest libraries in the ancient world was in Alexandria, Egypt.

Harvard College opened America's first library in 1638. The first public library in America was in Charleston, South Carolina. It opened in 1698, and local laws allowed anyone to "have liberty to borrow any book." In 1731, Benjamin Franklin created the Library Company in Philadelphia. He hired Louis Timothee, who was essentially America's first librarian. In 1802, John Beckley was named the first Librarian of Congress. The first children's library opened in Salisbury, Connecticut, in 1803.

Until 1833, libraries were set up by private individuals or clubs. That year, the city of Peterborough, New Hampshire, voted for public funds to create the first free public library.

Fictional Facts

You know the difference between fiction and nonfiction, right? Those two types of writing make up nearly all the books you might run across. For instance, this book is nonfiction because it contains facts and real-life information. Harry Potter *and other imaginary stories are fiction. Here are some fun fiction firsts:*

●◆ First novel: The description of a novel as a "long work of fiction" is pretty general, so it's hard to pin down the very first. Many experts say it is a Japanese work called *Genji-Monogatari*, written by a woman named Murasaki Shikibu in about 1000. The first novel in English . . . well, that's also a bit of a debate. One popular choice would be *Robinson Crusoe*, written by Daniel Defoe in 1719. It had most of the elements of a novel as it is recognized today.

●◆ The first novel written by a person born in America was *The Life of Harriot Stuart* by Charlotte Lennox in 1751.

●◆ The first historical novel (set in the distant past, often using real historical people as characters) is considered *Waverley* by Sir Walter Scott in 1814.

●◆ Detective stories are some of the most popular works of fiction. American author Edgar Allan Poe is considered the author of the first one, called "The Murders in the Rue Morgue." It was published in 1841.

●◆ Paperbacks are a handy way to make a book. They're lightweight, easy to carry, and less expensive than hardcovers. The first paperback book was called *Pelham*, an 1841 novel by Edward Bulwer-Lytton of England.

THE FIRST...

1

Letter

That would be "A," of course. It's a letter, it's a word ("a"), it's a great grade, it's "for apple." A has been a part of our English-language alphabet for, well, as long as we've had a complete English alphabet, which is about 700 years. Before that, it led off the Greek and Roman alphabets:

1 The sound of A comes first from the Hebrew word "aleph" (which means ox).

2 The shape of the letter is based on a "pictogram" (picture-letter) that was meant to look like the horns of an ox.

3 Only two words in the dictionary start with "aa": aardvark and aardwolf.

4 The Roman word for the letter A was "alpha" and for the letter B was "beta," from which we get the word "alphabet."

➤ The first fiction bestseller in America was a novel called *Uncle Tom's Cabin*, written in 1852 by Harriet Beecher Stowe.

➤ Like science fiction? Thank author Jules Verne. His 1864 book, *Journey to the Center of the Earth*, is recognized as the first science fiction novel.

➤ The first children's book to reach the number-one spot on *The New York Times*'s Bestseller List was *Harry Potter and the Goblet of Fire*.

Made in America

The first book written in America was A True Relation of Such Occurrences and Accidents of Noate as Hath Hapned in Virginia Since the First Planting of That Collony . . . , *by John Smith in 1608. The book (which was actually longer than its title) told stories of the first English settlement in America. Here are some other American book firsts:*

For the first couple of hundred years in America, schoolchildren used books called primers. These helped them learn the basics of letters, numbers, and other concepts. The *first primer*, the *New England Primer*, was issued in 1689.

The *first dictionary for Americans* was written in 1788 . . . by an Englishman! William Perry put together the *Royal Standard English Dictionary, Carefully Revised and Corrected*.

The *first dictionary by an American* came in 1806 when Noah Webster published his first dictionary. Webster's remains an important name in the dictionary world; we used one of its editions for spell-checking the *Scholastic Book of Firsts*!

People who have vision problems or are blind were shut out from reading books for a long time. In 1833, a Philadelphia school for the blind published part of the Bible using an early form of raised lettering. The *first books using the Braille alphabet* were released in Paris, France, in 1829 (and in America in 1859). Braille uses a series of raised dots to represent characters. In 1934, the *first recorded books* were produced on vinyl albums so that blind people could listen to books.

Comic Book #1s

In 1904, books filled with comic strips were published for the first time. The comic strips that had been printed in newspapers were then gathered into a book. The first comic book of original material was called New Fun Comics and was published in 1935.

The first comic-book superhero was Superman, who appeared for the first time in Action Comics #1 in June 1938. Superman was created by Jerry Siegel and Joe Shuster, two high school students from Ohio.

Here are the first appearances of some other famous comic book heroes:

HERO	COMIC TITLE	YEAR
Batman	Detective Comics #27	1939
Captain America	Captain America #1	1941
Aquaman	More Fun Comics #73	1941
Flash	Showcase #4	1956
Supergirl	Action Comics #252	1959
Fantastic Four	Fantastic Four #1	1961
Incredible Hulk	Incredible Hulk #1	1962
Spider-Man	Amazing Fantasy #15	1962
X-Men	X-Men #1	1963
Daredevil	Daredevil #1	1964
Wolverine	Incredible Hulk #180	1974
Sandman	Sandman #1	1989

Showtime! Music Firsts

Music has been around since human beings first tried to do something other than talk. Heck, you could say it's been around since the first bird tweeted. Here are some interesting firsts from the history of music:

♪ A harp dating to about 4500 BCE is regarded by some experts as the first musical instrument.

♪ The style known as "chamber music" was first played in Germany in the 1450s. For the first time, small groups played music in people's homes without a conductor.

♪ The first opera was performed in Florence, Italy, in 1597. It was called *Dafne*, and was written by Jacopo Peri.

♪ Free music! Until 1672, it was all free. That year, however, for the first time, violinist John Banister of England put on a concert and charged people money to listen.

♪ Orchestra conductors usually wave a small white stick called a baton. They didn't always, though. In 1780, Germany's Anselm Weber became the first to use a baton. Before that, conductors just waved their arms and hands.

♪ Quiz time: What instrument did Antoine Sax of Belgium invent in 1846? Hint: It wasn't the Antoinephone!

♪ The song "Yankee Doodle" was played on a cornet by Jules Levy in 1878. What's the big deal? Levy was recorded while playing, making it the first known musical recording.

Hall of Fame Firsts

Several music styles have halls of fame that honor pioneers and leaders in their type of music. Here are the first members (or inductees) of three music halls of fame:

Country Music Hall of Fame (Nashville, Tennessee): (1961) Jimmie Rodgers, Fred Rose, Hank Williams, Sr.

American Jazz Hall of Fame (Rutgers, New Jersey): (1983) Louis Armstrong, Count Basie, Bix Beiderbecke, Benny Carter, Duke Ellington, Dizzy Gillespie, Benny Goodman, Earl Hines, Jelly Roll Morton, Charlie Parker, Art Tatum

Rock and Roll Hall of Fame (Cleveland, Ohio): (1986) Chuck Berry, James Brown, Ray Charles, Sam Cooke, Fats Domino, The Everly Brothers, Alan Freed, John Hammond, Buddy Holly, Robert Johnson, Jerry Lee Lewis, Sam Phillips, Elvis Presley, Little Richard, Jimmie Rodgers, Jimmy Yancey

🎵 Music without people! The first player piano was patented by John McTammany of Massachusetts in 1881. A player piano uses a rotating drum of paper to control which notes are played.

🎵 The people who play music for you on radio stations are often called DJs or disk jockeys. The first DJ was Dr. Elman Myers, whose 18-hour (!) shows began broadcasting in 1911.

🎵 Who's number one? Music fans are always interested in what song or album is outselling the competition. In 1913, *Billboard* magazine published its first charts of top sellers.

🎵 Adolph Rickenbacker invented the electric guitar in 1935.

🎵 The first music video played on MTV when it started in 1981 was "Video Killed the Radio Star" by the Buggles.

Big Sellers

Music is produced in songs and as collections of songs, called albums (whether those are on vinyl disks or CDs). Beginning in 1941, any record (single song or album) that sold one million copies earned a special Gold Record award. The idea was born to honor the millionth sale of the song "Chattanooga Choo-Choo," by the Glenn Miller Orchestra in 1941.* Miller received a record album that had been gold-plated. Since 1975, a single song "goes gold" when it sells one million copies, while an album is golden when it sells 500,000 copies. If your single sells two million, you're platinum (that's better than gold, trust us); if you're an album, you only have to sell one million to earn platinum status. Here are some top-selling highlights:

First gold record (album): *Oklahoma!* from the Broadway musical, 1949

First rock 'n' roll gold album: *Shake, Rattle & Roll*, Bill Haley and the Comets, 1954

First gold record (single): "Catch a Falling Star," by Perry Como, 1958

First gold solo album: Harry Belafonte's *Calypso*, 1959

First female gold: *Judy Garland at Carnegie Hall*, 1961

First platinum song: "Disco Lady," by Johnny Taylor, 1976

First platinum album: *The Eagles: Their Greatest Hits 1971–75*, 1975

*Some record books say a 1912 recording by Al Jolson ("Ragging Baby to Sleep") sold more than two million copies, making it the first to reach "gold" sales levels. Several other recordings reached that level before the official awards were started in 1941.

Grammy Firsts

The Recording Industry Association of America hands out the most coveted trophies in music: the Grammys. Each winner gets a gold statue of an old-fashioned gramophone (that's where they get the name of the award), an early type of record player (see page 61 for more). The first Grammys were given out in 1959 and new categories have been added over the years to show how musical tastes have changed. Here are some firsts from Grammy history:

First Album of the Year: *The Music from Peter Gunn*, by Henry Mancini, 1959

First Record of the Year: *Nel Blu Dipinto di Blu (Volare)*, Domenico Modugno, 1959

First Best New Artist: Bob Newhart, 1961

First Best Country Song: "Dang Me," Roger Miller, 1965

First Best R&B Performance: "Hold It Right There," Ramsey Lewis, 1965

First Best Rock Performance (group): "Heartache Tonight," The Eagles, 1980

First Best Music Video (short form): "Hungry Like the Wolf," Duran Duran, 1984

First Best Alternative Music Performance: *I Do Not Want What I Haven't Got*, Sinéad O'Connor, 1991

First Best Pop Album: *Longing in Their Hearts*, Bonnie Raitt, 1995

First Best R&B Album: *II*, Boyz II Men, 1995

Rap and Hip-Hop

The musical styles known as rap and hip-hop quickly became enormously popular, especially with young audiences. The firsts in this category are sometimes hard to pin down, since so many people had a hand in creating these styles.

First rap song: Many artists were creating different kinds of poetry, rap, and musical stories in the 1970s. In 1979, the song "Rapper's Delight" by the Sugarhill Gang was released and was the first to bring this emerging music to a wide audience.

First gold rap album: *Run-D.M.C.* by the group of the same name, 1984

First rap movie: *Krush Groove*, released in 1985, featured Run-D.M.C. acting and performing.

First rap song to win a Grammy: In 1989, the Grammy Awards created a category for Best Rap Performance. Groups or solo artists were eligible (they received separate awards beginning in 1991). The first rap Grammy was won for the song "Parents Just Don't Understand" by DJ Jazzy Jeff & The Fresh Prince. The Fresh Prince, of course, is now better known as international superstar actor Will Smith.

First rapper to win a lifetime achievement award: Proving how much rap and hip-hop have become a vital part of music, the rap pioneer LL Cool J was given the 1997 MTV Video Vanguard Award for his nearly 20 years of performance and innovation.

Music Technology

Musicians make music, but people need a way to listen to it. Here are the firsts that helped teach the world to sing . . . or at least listen! (For radio firsts, see page 272.)

First recordings: Thomas Edison used wax cylinders to capture sound. He called his 1877 invention the phonograph.

First gramophone: In 1887, Emile Berliner did Edison one better with a gramophone that used wax discs to record and play back sound.

First albums: Berliner's first record albums spun 78 times per minute to produce sound. In 1933, RCA Victor Co. made the first 33.3 rpm (revolutions, or spins, per minute) albums, which became the standard. In 1948, Columbia Recordings made the first vinyl albums, which are still produced today.

First cassette tapes: Different versions of recording tape were invented beginning in 1928; the cassette tape format was introduced in 1963.

First CDs: The first compact discs, or CDs, were created by Japanese and Dutch companies in 1980. CD players went on sale in Japan in 1982 and in the United States a year later.

First DVDs: The first DVDs, or digital video discs, were created by several companies at once and announced in 1995.

First MP3: This handy digital music format was developed by several companies, along with Germany's Fraunhofer Institute for Integrated Circuits. The current standard was approved in 1997.

First Hits

Here are the first solo albums released by some famous performers. We tossed in a couple of pretty big-time music groups as well. Sorry if we missed your favorite!

ARTIST	ALBUM	YEAR
The Beatles	*Please Please Me*	1963
Beyoncé	*Dangerously in Love*	2003
Lil' Bow Wow	*Beware of Dog*	2000
Aaron Carter	*Aaron Carter*	1998
Faith Hill	*Take Me As I Am*	1993
Alicia Keys	*Songs in A Minor*	2001
Avril Lavigne	*Let Go*	2002
Jennifer Lopez	*On the 6*	1999
Madonna	*Madonna*	1983
Tim McGraw	*Tim McGraw*	1992
Nelly	*Country Grammar*	2000
Jessica Simpson	*Sweet Kisses*	1999
Britney Spears	*Baby One More Time*	1999

CHAPTER 3

Everyday Things

Look all around your house and you can find firsts. No, we don't mean the first time you cleaned up your room (still waiting for that, right?). We mean inventions and firsts that you probably can't imagine living without.

In the Kitchen

Humans have come a long way from lighting a fire and holding a hunk of meat over it. Cooking, usually in the kitchen, has been greatly helped by a number of key inventions. Here are a few:

First Oven

Cooking fires are as old as fire itself. Various structures, including fireplaces, were used to contain fires. These acted as early ovens. The key was to create something that could be used safely inside. Inventors often tried a "range," in which coal or wood was burned inside a metal box. The fire heated the top of the box, on which one could cook. In 1802, George Bodley made the first successful "modern" oven, which cooked inside the box instead of on top. The next big innovation was changing from coal or wood to gas or electricity as the heat source.

● The first meal cooked in a gas oven was in 1802, by German inventor Frederick Albert Winson.

● The first practical gas ovens for the home were sold in England in 1836.

● Electric ovens were first used in a Swiss hotel in 1889.

First Toaster

The first electric toaster was made in 1910 by Westinghouse Co. However, it was little more than a heated wire that sizzled the bread on one side. You had to watch the toast and grab it before it burned. In 1918, Charles Strite saved the world from burnt toast by inventing the pop-up toaster. He found a way for the temperature control to signal the pop-up device when the toast was done. Restaurants used his machines first; the home "Toastmaster" debuted in 1926. The public loved it so much that in 1927, March was named National Toaster Month to spread the word.

First Blender

Fred Waring invented the blender in 1936. He probably made the first milk shake five minutes later! In 1973, Carl Sontheimer invented the food processor called a Cuisinart.

First Refrigerator

Today, a refrigerator is the biggest thing in most kitchens. But back in 1803, the first device called a "refrigerator" was simply a two-layered box. Ice and food were stored together, with the ice keeping the food cold. The key to a "real" refrigerator is a device called a compressor. A compressor cools heated air and then uses it to cool the stuff inside the fridge. In 1834, Jacob Perkins put a compressor on an icebox, but since it had to be cranked by hand to work, it wasn't too popular. When people figured out how to get electricity to run compressors, inventors returned to the idea of refrigeration.

In 1913, the Domelre refrigerator sold for $900 and became the first electric fridge for home use. In 1934, General Electric created the first quiet compressor and sold the first popular home refrigerator. Cold food lovers everywhere rejoiced!

First Aluminum Cookware

For centuries, iron formed most cookware. Today, most pots and pans are made of aluminum, which is a lighter metal than iron. In 1886, Charles Martin Hall perfected the first aluminum pans, selling them as the "Wear-Ever" brand.

Cleaning Up

First Vacuum Cleaner

Not that you ever use one (your mom would be stunned!) but cleaners around the world were thrilled when Hubert Cecil Booth patented a "suction cleaning device" in 1901. It wasn't exactly portable—Booth's first vacuum was on a wagon and long hoses were pushed into a house to suck up the dirt. An American janitor named James Spangler made a smaller version in 1907, one that a person could actually carry around while cleaning up. His brother-in-law, William Hoover, bought Spangler's invention and, well, he cleaned up. The Hoover Vacuum Company's products became so popular that a new word was created: To "hoover" means to use suction to pick up objects.

First Washer and Dryer

Just as fire has been part of cooking for millennia, so, too, has water been the way to clean things. Clothes especially were washed in water, but this was very labor-intensive. Many inventors looked for a way to make this job easier. The first American patent for a machine that cleaned clothes by tumbling them around and around (via a hand crank) was awarded to Hamilton Smith in 1858. The first electric clothes washer was the Thor, sold in 1907. It worked, but Mom—er, the user—still had to open it several times to put in detergent or turn on the rinse cycle. In 1937, the first automatic washer was invented by John Chamberlain; with this model, folks put in clothes and soap and just pushed a button.

But all the clothes were still wet after washing. Hanging them outside worked, but not in bad weather. J. Ross Moore of North Dakota, famous for its long, cold winters, came up with a way to spin clothes over a flame or a heater. The Hamilton Company perfected his ideas and sold the first clothes dryers in 1938.

Detergent vs. Soap

Soap made from animal fats has been around for thousands of years. However, that type of soap leaves a thin, goopy film on things it cleans. In the 1890s, German scientists discovered detergents, a kind of soap that doesn't use animal fats. These chemicals were perfect for washing dishes and clothes, since they rinsed completely away with water.

First Dishwasher

In 1886, Josephine Cochrane, an American woman looking for a way to make her home life simpler, invented an electric dishwashing machine. It won the highest technical award at the Chicago World's Fair in 1893. A home version was made in 1914.

First Teflon

More good news for people who wash dishes came in 1938, when Teflon, a super nonsticky substance that made cleaning pots and pans a snap, was invented accidentally by Roy Plunkett of DuPont.

In the Bathroom

First Toilet Paper

Before someone finally figured this one out, here are some of the things people used as TP: wool, corncobs, mussel shells, pages from a book (in America, often the Sears catalog), coconut shells (ouch!), lace, a sponge soaked in salt water on the end of a stick, and moss. So, hooray for the Scott brothers, Edward and Clarence, whose company mass-produced America's first rolls of toilet paper in 1879. (Joseph Gayetty had tried and failed to sell huge boxes of thin sheets in 1857. At the same time as the Scotts, inventor Walter Alcock could not convince the British public to buy his rolls.) But the Scotts kept the product rolling, so to speak, and made it into what some people call the one thing they could not imagine doing without!

Other Bathroom Stuff:

➤➤ Paper towels (1907): This kind of paper product from the Scott Paper Co. was a hit because it was the first to be strong, but still flexible enough to be rolled up.

➤➤ Kleenex tissues (1914): The Scott Paper Co. created a product called cellucotton but then didn't know what to do with it. Nurses working in Europe in 1914 used it to clean their patients or wipe up spills. It proved to be strong and absorbent. In smaller sheets, it became the perfect facial tissue paper.

➤➤ Pop-up tissue box (1921): Once they had Kleenex, this became the easiest way to go from box to nose.

▶▶ Q-tips (1925): Leo Gerstenzang watched his wife try to wrap cotton around a toothpick to clean their baby's ears and thought, "There's got to be a better way." There was.

The First Toilets

Have a seat and read about the invention of the modern toilet. For centuries, people went far from their own buildings to places called outhouses. These were usually little huts built over holes in the ground—sounds comfy, huh? Some large buildings, such as castles, had special rooms for, well, you know. (In castles, this was often a room high up on an outside wall. When a person sat down, there was nothing below them except a nice view of the ground far below.) Later, chamberpots were used indoors, but had to be emptied (often!) outside.

None of these methods, however, used water to wash away the waste. In 1596, an Englishman named Sir John Harrington drew up the first plans for an indoor toilet that used a water tank to flush. The tank was on a wall above the toilet bowl. Queen Elizabeth I put one in her palace that year, but Harrington had not solved the problem of odors rising up from the toilet.

In 1775, Alexander Cummings came to the rescue. He invented the S-curve pipe. This holds a little bit of water in it at all times, so that odors can't come back up through the bowl. As great as that sounds, it took another 125 years before indoor flushing toilets were nearly standard in American and British homes.

Tooth Stuff

You brush twice a day and use floss every day, right? (Well, almost every day. . . .) The stuff you use to clean your teeth had to start somewhere . . . and here is where:

First toothbrushes: The first known bristle-brush toothbrush was made in China in the late 1400s. The sharp hairs of hogs were used for the bristles. In Europe a century later, people tried horsehair and badger hair. The invention of chemical-based nylon in the 1930s led to the first nylon brush in 1938. It was sold as Dr. West's Miracle Tuft Toothbrush. No word on who Dr. West was. The first electric toothbrush was the Broxodent model sold in 1961.

First dental floss: Some archaeologists say that toothpicks have been around for nearly two million years! But dental floss is a relative newcomer. In 1819, Levi Spear Parmly created a waxed silk thread for cleaning between teeth. Today, dental floss is made of synthetic materials.

First toothpaste: Ancient Egyptians and Greeks had recipes for teeth-cleaning substances. The Egyptians included rust, while Hippocrates of Greece tossed in ground mice and rabbit heads (ew!). Modern chemistry has come up with better choices since then. The first toothpaste put into the familiar tubes was Dr. Sheffield's Crème Dentifrice in 1892. The packaging idea came from the tubes used to sell artists' paints.

The biggest news in toothpaste came in 1915 when scientists showed that adding a chemical called fluoride to the paste helped create healthy teeth. Now, most toothpastes contain fluoride.

Hair on Your Face

Most of you don't have to worry about shaving yet. But you may someday (trust us!). Here are some firsts from the world of shaving:

First safety razor: King Gillette worked with several partners to create the first disposable razor blade in 1903. Users kept the handle of the razor, but replaced the small, thin square blades when they got dull.

First electric razor: Jacob Schick invented the rotating-head electric razor in 1923, and it first went on sale in 1931. With it, people could shave without using water or shaving cream.

First multiblade razor: In 1971, the twin-bladed safety razor was introduced. A third blade was added in 1999. As of 2004, shavers could also choose a mighty four-bladed razor!

First razor for women: Gillette sold a razor designed specifically for women beginning in 1915.

SAY IT FIRST...

first aid Immediate medical help given after a person is hurt. Most first aid can be performed by people who are not doctors, nurses, or EMTs. The Red Cross offers training, even for kids, on basic first aid.

Being Beautiful

For thousands of years, people have been trying to improve their appearance with all sorts of makeup. Ancient Egyptians used eyeliner made from ground-up plants such as kohl or minerals like malachite. European women in the Middle Ages powdered their faces with arsenic, which turned out to be poisonous! French ladies of the 1800s stuck small paper "beauty spots" on their faces. So it's hard to say when some of the world's favorite makeups were first used. However, we've tracked down a few things about the world of beauty that did have a first place:

❋ **Vaseline**, a petroleum jelly (that means it's made from the same stuff as oil for your car!) was invented in 1870 by Robert Chesebrough.

❋ **ChapStick** lip balm debuted in 1884.

❋ Though no one would talk about it at the time, the first underarm **antiperspirant**, named Mum, was marketed in 1888.

❋ **Shampoo** was developed in the 1890s in Germany.

❋ The first **hair coloring** cream was sold in 1907 in France. In 1956, Miss Clairol became the first in-home hair dye that was also a shampoo.

❋ *Transparent liquid nail polishes* were first created in 1907; the first colored polish was sold in 1917 (it was pink).

❋ The first **cold cream** to be made of oils suspended in water—the first not to use animal fats—was Nivea, made by Herman Beiersdorf in 1911.

❋ *Lipstick* was first packaged in its familiar sliding tube in 1915.

❋ The **electric hair dryer** debuted in 1920, created at the same time by two companies in Racine, Wisconsin.

❋ The famous perfume *Chanel No. 5* was released on May 5, 1921, by Coco Chanel. (May 5...5/5, get it?)

❋ Thank former president of Israel Chaim Weizmann for inventing a process in 1910 that led to the creation of acetone as a *nail-polish remover*.

❋ Max Factor was a cosmetics pioneer who popularized many forms of makeup. One of his greatest was a water-soluble *"foundation" powder*, first sold in 1938.

❋ *Aerosol hairspray* was first sold in the United States in 1949; today's hairsprays do not use aerosol, which contains environmentally unfriendly chemicals called CFCs.

Dressing a Kid

Believe it or not, kids have been wearing pretty much the same basic stuff—jeans, T-shirts, sneakers—for what seems like forever. But it's actually been less than 100 years. Still, although fashions change, and new styles and clothing products come up all the time, you're a rare kid who doesn't wear some of these items at least once in a while. Here's how the big three got their start:

First Sneakers

The first step was the invention of "vulcanized" or hardened rubber in the 1860s by Charles Goodyear (yep, the tire guy). Though Goodyear sold shoes like sneakers, the first real brand of sneakers was Keds, first sold in 1917. They had canvas tops and rubber bottoms. The next big innovation was the waffle-patterned sole, sold by Phil Knight and Bill Bowerman of Nike, beginning in 1962. In 1967, nylon was first used as the top part of sneakers.

First Jeans

Thank a man named Levi Strauss for this indispensable part of our wardrobe. While outfitting hardy miners in

California in the 1850s, he looked for a sturdy fabric. He found it in denim (so called after the French name for it, *serge de Nîmes*), also called jeans (after a textile made for sailors in Genoa called Genes). Dying it indigo blue, Strauss put his first name on the product and had an instant hit. The familiar metal rivets were first added in 1873.

First T-Shirt

Undershirts with short sleeves (or no sleeves) had been worn by men for many years until 1942. That year, the U.S. Navy issued patterns for its official short-sleeved undershirt. The form stuck and by the end of World War II, the T-shirt had become okay to wear on its own.

Swim Time

✦ The first swimsuit made from stretchy fabric (as opposed to heavy wool) was made in Portland, Oregon, in 1915 by Carl Jantzen.

✦ The first bikini was shown in public on July 5, 1946. It got its name from Bikini Atoll in the Pacific Ocean, where the first nuclear bomb had been tested just a few days earlier. The garment was designed by Frenchman Louis Reard.

✦ Surf trunks known as Birdies were first made in 1959.

Sticking Clothes Together

👉 The oldest buttons ever found were from an archaeological dig in India dating to 2000 BCE.

👉 The zipper was invented in 1893 by Whitcomb Judson, using metal hooks and eyes.

👉 The modern zipper, using jagged interlocking metal teeth, was created in 1913 by Gideon Sundback.

👉 Walter Hunt invented the modern version of the safety pin in 1849. He then sold the patent rights for the device for only $100. Oops.

Velcro!

Velcro, that fantastic sticky stuff that is probably part of a dozen things you own, first made its appearance in 1951. Velcro was invented by George de Mestral of Switzerland. A hiking fan, he saw how seeds stuck to his dog's fur and tried to make cloth that did the same thing. The name comes from French. "Vel" comes from *velour*, meaning "velvet," and "cro" from the French word *crochet* for "hook."

The Eyes Have It

Though people have had bad eyesight ever since there have been people, eyeglasses (or at least the corrective lenses to look through) were only first created around 1280, in the Italian town of Pisa (two different people claimed the invention). The first spectacles with temple pieces (before then all eyeglasses perched on one's nose) were sold in 1727 by Edward Scarlett. Benjamin Franklin is credited for popularizing bifocals, that is, lenses that aid with both close-up and distance viewing.

Closet Firsts

>> Button-down shirt collars for men were created by John Brooks in 1900. So thank John the next time your mom makes you dress up to see Aunt Millie.

>> The tuxedo was first worn at Tuxedo Park, New York (from which it got its name), in 1886.

>> Though carried for many years, beginning as far back as Roman times, umbrellas were considered only suitable for women. Jonas Hanway of England began to carry one daily beginning in 1750. His practice caught on, and by the time he died in 1786, carrying an umbrella was part of the British male "uniform."

>> A Scotsman named Charles Macintosh created a way to combine sheets of thin rubber with cloth to create a waterproof fabric that he used to make the first raingear.

>> British designer Mary Quant shocked the world by selling the first miniskirts in 1965.

Toy Stories

C'mon admit it . . . you still play with tons of toys. Well, you're not alone. Toys have thrilled kids for thousands of years. Some of today's toys have been around for decades, while others are more recent. Here is a list of the first year that some popular toys were sold:

TOY	YEAR FIRST SOLD
Plasticine (modeling clay)	1897
Silly Putty	1943
Slinky	1945
Frisbee	1948*
LEGO	1958
Hula-Hoop	1958
Barbie	1959
Ken	1961
G.I. Joe	1964
Hello Kitty	1974
Rubik's Cube	1975
Strawberry Shortcake	1980
Cabbage Patch Kids	1983
Transformers	1984
Beanie Babies	1993
Power Rangers	1993
Bionicles	2002

*First called "Morrison's Flyin' Saucer"—not called Frisbee until 1958

Note: All names of toys and games are registered trademarks of their respective owners. See page 2.

Cuddly Teddy

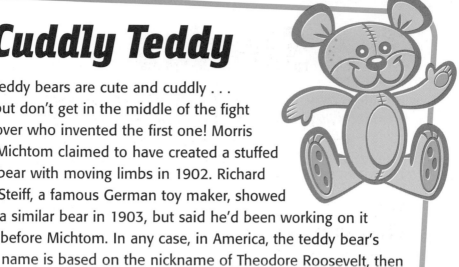

Teddy bears are cute and cuddly . . . but don't get in the middle of the fight over who invented the first one! Morris Michtom claimed to have created a stuffed bear with moving limbs in 1902. Richard Steiff, a famous German toy maker, showed a similar bear in 1903, but said he'd been working on it before Michtom. In any case, in America, the teddy bear's name is based on the nickname of Theodore Roosevelt, then president of the United States.

Hoop It Up!

A Hula-Hoop is a large circular tube filled with beads. When you swivel it around your hips, the beads create a nice swishing sound. Hula-Hoops were first sold in 1958, and the first swishing sound they made was caused by its inventors counting all their money! Richard Knerr and Spud Melin of the Wham-O Company were inspired by Australian gym teachers using wooden hoops in class. The two men brought the idea to America but used plastic instead. Almost overnight, Hula-Hoops were everywhere! They were what is called a "fad," which means something that many people are just crazy about for a short time. In just a few months, more than 20 million Hula-Hoops were sold in the United States. The fad faded soon after, but Hula-Hoops are still around . . . and around . . . and around!

Great Games!

Slow down, reader. Put down your mouse, your joystick, and your control pad. It's time to talk about board games here . . . the ones you play when the power is out or your parents say you're playing too many video games! (Check out page 282 for great video game firsts.)

GAME	YEAR FIRST SOLD
Game of Life	1866
Chutes and Ladders	1870
Tiddlywinks	1888
Scrabble	1931
Monopoly	1933
Sorry!	1934
Candyland	1949
Risk	1959
Stratego	1960
Battleship	1967
Mastermind	1970
Uno	1971
Dungeons and Dragons	1973
Trivial Pursuit	1979
Magic: The Gathering	1993

Boards and Blades

Your parents putted around on scooters and clay-wheel skateboards. Things have gotten a lot more intense since then, but here's how some of today's extreme sports gear got started. (Check out our Sports chapter for more firsts in skateboarding.)

First roller skates: Made by Joseph Merlin of Belgium in 1759, with two wheels. Four-wheeled skates with a brake pad were patented by James Plimpton of New York in 1863.

First in-line skates: Looking for a way to play hockey when there was no ice, Minnesota brothers Scott and Brennan Olson lined up the wheels on their roller skates, and, ta-dah, in-line skating was born in 1979.

First skateboards: The first boards were created in California in the 1950s. Kids put roller-skate wheels on boards and "surfed" the sidewalks. In 1959, Bill Richards sold what are considered by some as the first commercial boards. The key first for skateboards came in 1973 when Frank Nasworthy invented urethane wheels. Softer and easier to turn on, yet more durable, urethane wheels became the only way to skate.

First snowboards: Jake Burton Carpenter created the first successful version of a snowboard in 1977, but he credits many others with helping develop the idea of "surfing" down a snowy hill.

In the Garden

No, we can't tell you when the first flower grew or who planted the first lawn. But we can tell you about some of the stuff you might find in your yard or garden:

First Lawn Mower

Edwin Budding made the first mechanical mower in 1830 in England; it was pulled by people or horses. The London Zoo bought the first one. Edwin George, an American Army officer, invented the first gas-powered lawn mower in 1919. Kids everywhere were thrilled that a weekly chore got a little bit easier! (Bonus first: The first U.S. Lawn Mower Racing championships were held in 1992.)

First Grass Seed

It doesn't grow by itself! Homeowners looking at their pride and joy can thank Orlando Mumford Scott, who sold the first weed-free grass seed in 1928. Scott also invented home-lawn fertilizer and chemical weed killer.

First Flower Seed

Well, no one actually invented flower seeds, of course. They came with the flowers (leading to the question which came first . . . the flower or the seed?). But in 1878 a man named

W. A. Burpee became the first to offer small packages of seeds, perfect for home gardeners.

First Wheelbarrow

No one knows who made the first wheelbarrow, but this handy device tells an interesting story about firsts. From what archaeologists can discover, the wheelbarrow was created at different times in two parts of the world. In China in about 200 CE, workers used a one-wheeled cart they called the "wooden ox." In Europe, people started with a two-wheeled cart as early as 1000 BCE, but eventually cut it to one wheel. Both places can claim they made the first wheelbarrows.

First Artificial Fertilizer

Fertilizers are products added to dirt to help plants grow. Most fertilizers come from, well, animals, mostly cows (that's right: cow poop). In 1859, James Mapes patented a formula made of lime and ammonia that did the same job . . . with less smell!

First Rubber Garden Hose

About 30 years after Charles Goodyear accidentally created a way to make things out of rubber, B. F. Goodrich started a company to make many rubber things. One of the first was a rubber garden hose, which went on sale in 1871.

School Days

Here are some firsts from the history of schools in America.
Don't worry—there will not be a quiz on this material.

YEAR   FIRST

???   First school in America: There's a bit of a debate—it might have been founded in 1620 in the Massachusetts or Virginia colonies. Other records say a Dutch school in New York City in 1633 was the first formal school for young children. The Boston Latin School, founded in 1635, is the oldest active school in America.

1642   First law to state that kids (younger than 11) have to go to school (Massachusetts)

1720   First school for Native-American kids (Virginia)

1807   First school for deaf students (New York City)

1820   First high school (Boston, Massachusetts)

1824   First public high school for girls (Worcester, Massachusetts)

1827   First nursery school (New York City)

1827   First free public schools (Massachusetts)

1829   First school for blind students (Boston, Massachusetts)

1846   First schools to group students into grades based on their ages (Quincy, Massachusetts)

1848 First school for children with mental disabilities (Boston, Massachusetts)

1850 First year that school became the rule for kids 6 to 14 nationwide

1853 First year that physical education was required in school (Boston, Massachusetts)

1860 First kindergarten, created by Elizabeth Peabody (Boston, Massachusetts)

1909 First junior high school (Columbus, Ohio)

1934 First driving classes in high school (State College, Pennsylvania)

1948 First school for performing arts (New York City)

School Stuff

First blackboards: Introduced to American schools by Christopher Dock of Pennsylvania in 1714. The wipe-off "whiteboards" were invented by WallTalkers Co. in 1993.

First pencils: No one knows for sure, but one first appeared in 1565 when Swiss scientist Konrad von Gesner put graphite in a wooden holder. Erasers were first added to the tops of pencils in 1858.

First handheld pencil sharpener: Invented by John Lee Love in 1897

First pens: The first ball-point pen was invented by Hungarian Laszlo Biro in 1938, but most of his models were expensive and often broke. The low-cost, more disposable BIC pen was first sold in France in 1953.

First tape: Masking tape was created by Richard Drew at 3M in 1925; cellophane tape was introduced in 1930.

First stapler: The first strips of metal staples were made by the Boston Wire Stitcher Co. in 1923.

MY FIRST...

The first school I attended was called _____

_____.

It was located in _____.

My first teacher was named _____.

_____ and _____

were my first friends at school.

Higher Education

Look out ahead . . . college is coming sooner than you think. Here are some interesting firsts from the world of higher education:

The ***first college in America*** was Harvard College, established in 1636 in Massachusetts. It was first called Cambridge College after the town it is in; it was renamed Harvard in 1638 as a tribute to John Harvard, who donated money and books to the college.

The ***first college to accept both male and female students*** was Oberlin Collegiate Institute, in Oberlin, Ohio, which opened in 1833. Up until then, all colleges were for men only.

In 1836, Mount Holyoke College opened in Massachusetts, becoming the ***first American college for women only***. Female-only Wesleyan College in Georgia opened in the same year.

African-American students were welcome only at a few schools in America until the Ashmun Institute opened in Pennsylvania in 1854. It was the ***first college for African Americans***. In 1866, Howard University was the first such institution for black students to offer professional degrees. (In 1823, Alexander Twilight had become the ***first African-American college graduate*** when he completed studies at Middlebury College in Vermont.)

The Navajo Community College, opened in 1969, was the ***first college on a Native American reservation***.

Got a Minute?

Check out these firsts from the world of clocks, watches, and other timepieces:

First Sundials

The oldest ever found were made in ancient Egypt in the 8th century BCE.

First Mechanical Clock

The first known clock that was NOT a sundial was made in China in 1088. It was a clock in which water flowed over a gear, lowering a weight at an even rate to record the passage of time.

First Clock with a Minute Hand

It was built in 1577 by Jost Bürgi in Switzerland, a country that would become famous for its clockmakers.

First Alarm Clock

Building on earlier inventions, Levi Hutchins made a mechanical alarm clock in 1787, but it only rang at 4 A.M.! In 1876, Seth Thomas received a patent for the first bedside alarm clock.

First Wristwatch

Philosopher Blaise Pascal was the first to strap a regular watch to his wrist in the late 1600s.

First Stopwatch

Swiss watchmaker Jean-Moise Pouzait created a way to "stop and start time" with his 1776 invention.

First Electric Clock

Alexander Bain and John Barwise invented a clock that ran on electricity in 1841.

First Waterproof Watch

Divers were thrilled with the introduction in 1926 of the Rolex Oyster, which would function when worn in up to 100 feet (33 m) of water.

First Atomic Clock

As scientists unlocked the secrets of the atom, they realized that atoms vibrated at precise rates (see below). The most precise clocks are atomic clocks. The first was invented in 1948 by Harold Lyons, based on the vibrations of an atom of ammonia.

First Digital Wristwatch

The 1971 Pulsar was the first watch with which people could tell time using digital numerals instead of hands.

Key Discovery!

In 1929, scientist Warren Marrison discovered that the mineral quartz always vibrated at a rate of exactly 32,768 times per second when an electric current passed through it. Using quartz crystals, time could be kept much more accurately than with gears, as in "regular" clocks and watches. At first, quartz clocks were used only in industry, but gradually the clocks got smaller and smaller until . . . the *first successful quartz wristwatch* was released to the public by Seiko in 1969.

THE FIRST...

Day of the Year

1

January 1 is, of course, the first day of each year. Here are some facts about this famous first:

✳ The first New Year's Day on January 1 was celebrated in 46 BCE, when the new "Julian" calendar was created and named for Roman general Julius Caesar.

✳ January is named for Janus, a Roman god of beginnings. Janus is pictured with two faces, one looking forward to the future and the other looking backward at the past.

✳ The song sung by many people as January 1 begins is called "Auld Lang Syne." That means "old long ago," and is based on a poem by Scottish poet Robert Burns.

✳ The biggest American celebration of New Year's Eve is in Times Square in New York City. Hundreds of thousands of people gather to watch a huge neon ball drop to the bottom of a pole located high above the street. When the ball reaches the bottom, a new year has begun.

✳ The Tournament of Roses Parade is held on January 1 each year in Pasadena, California, except when the day falls on a Sunday. Early parade organizers feared that all the hoopla of the parade would startle horses who were waiting outside Pasadena's churches!

✳ In Ecuador, celebrants write down a list of other people's faults, then build scarecrows to frighten away those faults.

✳ In Madagascar, people pour water on themselves to start the New Year fresh.

✳ Traditional New Year's Day foods include black-eyed peas, sauerkraut, and pancakes.

✳ Paul Revere, Betsy Ross, and author J. D. Salinger were all born on January 1.

✳ On January 1, 1863, President Abraham Lincoln issued the Emancipation Proclamation.

CHAPTER 4

Exploration

It's a big world . . . someone has to explore it all. This chapter is a salute to the first people—from all around the globe—who bravely discovered the answers to the question, "Just what the heck is out there, anyway?"

Who Came First?

Originally, many students were taught that Italian sailor Christopher Columbus was the first person to land in America or that British explorer David Livingstone was the first to discover Victoria Falls in Africa. Now we know better. Columbus and Livingstone risked their lives and their reputations in the name of exploration, and their achievements cannot be ignored. But of course they weren't really the first people to view those sights—they were the first from Europe!

Remember, there were people living on the Caribbean islands when Columbus landed on them, and people living along the Zambezi River when Livingstone got there. For many years, historians didn't pay much attention to these folks. Now we have a better understanding of who those people were and how important they are to the story of their homelands.

Still, European pioneers like Columbus are important historical figures. For one thing, they are often the first documented visitors to various lands. (By documented, we mean something written down for later generations to read and study.) For another, it was the Europeans who launched the great Age of Exploration in the 15th century. As explorers from Europe began to sail the world and map its features, the earth gradually became more accessible and united.

Discovery and exploration continue today. In this chapter, you'll go along on some of those adventurous treks to create firsts from all over the globe: on the ocean and on raging rivers; 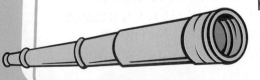 high atop snowy mountains; from the top and bottom of the world; and everywhere in between.

Mapping the Globe

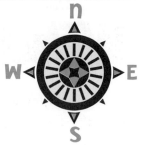

As people traveled away from their homelands over the centuries, they wanted to record where they had been. First, so they could prove where they had gone, and second, so others could follow. By creating maps, they could better understand their surroundings. Here are some map firsts:

First known map: A Babylonian clay tablet found at Nuzi, Iraq, and dating from around 2300 BCE, now on exhibit at the Semitic Museum of Harvard in Cambridge, Massachusetts

First world map: Most experts say it's the work of the Greek philosopher and astronomer Anaximander of Miletus (he lived in what is today Turkey), who engraved a circular map of the known world on a stone tablet about 550 BCE.

First globe that still exists: A hollow shell, about 20 inches (51 cm) in diameter, made by German mapmaker Martin Behaim and completed in 1492

First map with the name "America" on it:
In 1507, by German cartographer Martin Waldseemüller. It was designed in 12 connected segments (sort of like sections of an orange) and made from a single wood block.

First map to be drawn, engraved, printed and published in the American colonies:
John Foster's woodcut of New England (1677). It became known as the "Wine Hills' Map" because the English edition mistakenly printed "Wine Hills" instead of "White Hills" in New Hampshire.

The New World

European explorers heading west across the Atlantic Ocean ran into the North American and South American continents. Since they were looking for India, they were rather surprised— or just confused! Here are some key firsts in the history of "New World" exploration:

✴ The first people from Europe to set foot on North America were probably Vikings led by Leif Ericsson. Many historians think he sailed to the coast of present-day Newfoundland, Canada, circa 1000.

✴ The first European city in the New World was Isabella, on the island now known as Hispaniola, founded 1493.

✴ After the Vikings, the first European to arrive on the North American continent was English explorer John Cabot, sailing under a charter from England's King Henry VII in 1497. Cabot landed at modern-day Newfoundland on June 24.

✴ In 1513, Spanish sailor Vasco de Balboa of Spain was the first European to sight the Pacific Ocean from North America. But he didn't sail there. Instead, he and his men hiked westward from the Atlantic Ocean across the Isthmus of Panama in 1513. When they got to the other side, Balboa reportedly waded into the surf and shouted, "By the grace of God, I claim all that sea and the countries bordering on it for the King and Castile!"

✴ Vitus Bering of Denmark was the first European to explore what is today the state of Alaska in 1741.

That Man Columbus

Was the man known as Christopher Columbus the first person to "discover" America? Well . . . no. Not only were millions of people living there, several other Europeans found parts of North America before he did. But Columbus was the first explorer to make it clear that rich and fertile lands lay across the ocean from Europe . . . lands much closer than India and Asia, which was what most folks thought was "out there."

The explorer was born Cristoforo Colombo in or near Genoa, Italy, in 1451. By the time King Ferdinand and Queen Isabella of Spain gave him money for ships in 1492, he was known as Christopher Columbus. At this time, most people still believed that China, India, and the Spice Islands lay across the ocean to the west of Europe.

On August 3, Columbus led a crew of about 90 sailors in three ships—*Niña*, *Pinta*, and the flagship, *Santa Maria*—westward in search of trade in Asia. After weeks on the open sea, the men finally spotted land. On October 12, Columbus landed on an island he named San Salvador, in what is now the Bahamas. He was the first to visit the Caribbean islands of Cuba, Haiti, Puerto Rico, Jamaica, Trinidad, and Martinique, as well as Venezuela. His exploration launched a wave of European colonization and changed the course of modern history. He wasn't first to America, but he was the first to make it *the* place to visit.

Three curious facts about Columbus:

1) He never set foot on the North American continent.

2) Even on his fourth voyage, he remained convinced that he was very close to India or China.

3) In 1498 he declared Earth to be pear-shaped rather than round.

Here Come the Europeans!

The race was on to find out more about this enormous continent. Explorers from many countries climbed into wooden sailing ships and headed west. Here are some of the travelers' first sightings of key North American places:

SITE	EXPLORER/COUNTRY OF ORIGIN/YEAR
Hudson River	Giovanni da Verrazano/Italy/1524
St. Lawrence River	Jacques Cartier/France/1534
Colorado River	Francisco de Ulloa/Spain/1539
Grand Canyon	García López de Cárdeñas/Spain/1540
Rio Grande	Francisco de Coronado/Spain/1540
Mississippi River	Hernando De Soto/Spain/1541
Lake Superior	Étienne Brulé/France/1622
Lake Michigan	Jean Nicolet/France/1634
Niagara Falls	Father Louis Hennepin/France/1678
Columbia River	Robert Gray/United States/1792
Mt. McKinley (Denali)	George Vancouver/England/1794

SITE	EXPLORER/COUNTRY OF ORIGIN/YEAR
Old Faithful Geyser	John Colter/United States/1807
Great Salt Lake	James Bridger/United States/1824
Mt. Whitney	Josiah D. Whitney/United States/1864

Settling In

Just taking a look at things was not enough, of course. After the explorers went home and described what they had seen, colonists followed to create towns and cities.

➤ The first permanent European settlement in America was St. Augustine, Florida, founded on September 8, 1565, by Don Pedro Menéndez of Spain.

➤ The first European settlement north of Florida was on Neutral Island at Calais, Maine, and was founded in 1604 by French explorer Pierre du Guast.

➤ The first permanent English settlement in America was in Jamestown, Virginia, founded May 13, 1607. Some 105 colonists arrived on the *Susan Constant*, *Godspeed*, and *Discovery*. A settlement at Roanoke, Virginia, mysteriously disappeared in 1590. That settlement did boast . . .

➤ . . . the first European person born in what would be the United States—Virginia Dare, born in 1587.

Sailing the Seas

The early explorers couldn't hop on a plane to get where they were going, of course. Instead, sailing ships carried them across the wide, open ocean on their way to . . . finding a place in this book! Here are some firsts in maritime exploring history:

First recorded seagoing voyage: Egyptian sailors traveled to Byblos (Phoenicia) in search of cedarwood in 2600 BCE.

First detailed account of a long sea voyage: *Ta peri okerinou (On the Ocean)*, by the Greek explorer and geographer Pytheas. He left Greece in 324 BCE, sailed through Gibraltar, circled Britain, visited Scandinavia and maybe even the Baltic Sea—some 8,000 miles (13,000 km).

Thanks, Wind!

Three exploring firsts were powered by storms:

The first Native Americans to cross the Atlantic may have been a group of men shipwrecked in Northern Europe (probably

SAY IT FIRST...

first mate On a ship, the person who is second in command after the captain. The first mate generally runs the sailing or steering of the ship, under the captain's orders.

Super Sailor

Sir Francis Drake of England was the first captain to complete a trip around the world. He left Plymouth, England, in 1577 with five ships, including his flagship, the *Golden Hind*, and 164 men. After going around South America, he sailed across the Pacific and reached the Spice Islands, known today as Indonesia. Drake then led his ships around the southern tip of Africa and then north toward Europe. On September 26, 1580, Drake returned in triumph to Plymouth—his ship was loaded with gold and jewels.

France) in 62 CE. They were probably fishermen from the Canadian or American coast who were blown out to sea in a storm.

The first European to reach Greenland was Gunnbjörn, a Norwegian Viking who was blown west by storms c. 930.

The first European to sail around the southern tip of Africa was Bartolomeu Dias of Portugal. In 1488, his ships were blown far to the south. Instead of heading back north, he sailed east, passing below the southern tip of Africa. He then turned north and sighted land on the east coast of Africa.

The First Looonnng Trip

In 1521, the Spanish ship *Victoria* became the first ship to sail around the world! On September 20, 1519, Ferdinand Magellan of Portugal left Spain with five ships, including the *Victoria*, and 270 men. After sailing past South America, Magellan's crew named the Pacific Ocean, because they didn't experience any storms while crossing it ("pacific" means "peaceful"). But Magellan didn't make the final trip home. He was killed in battle on the Philippine islands. In 1521, the *Victoria* and 18 crewmen made it home as the first global circumnavigators.

North Pole

The ice cap at the top of the world has mesmerized explorers for centuries. The forbidding, cold, and isolated landscape makes it terribly dangerous to explore. But many hardy travelers completed these firsts:

First to sail into the Arctic Ocean: Vitus Bering of Denmark in 1728, through what came to be called the Bering Strait, proving that Asia and North America are not joined by land

First European explorer to reach the Arctic by land from North America: Samuel Hearne, a British fur trader employed by the Hudson's Bay Co. who arrived at the mouth of the Coppermine River in 1770

First woman to join a polar expedition: Josephine Peary, wife of Robert (below), who sailed with him in the *Kite* in 1891

First to go under the North Pole: The U.S. nuclear submarine *Nautilus*, remaining submerged during the entire trip, sailed under the Pole on August 3, 1958.

Polar-izing Debate

Who was the first person to reach the North Pole? Two men claimed the title. Robert Peary said he got there first on April 6, 1909. Four Eskimos and an African-American assistant, Matthew Henson, traveled with Peary by dogsled. Soon after Peary's return, Frederick Cook claimed he had reached the Pole on April 21, 1908. Scientists and journalists have debated for years, with some saying that neither man actually reached the real North Pole!

South Pole

At the other end of the earth is the continent of Antarctica, home of the South Pole. It, too, has been the site of several centuries' worth of exploring firsts:

First to spot the Antarctic mainland: Three
explorers, each sailing on different expeditions, all claimed to be the first in 1820. No one is sure who was really the first: 1) Russian Fabian von Bellingshausen 2) Englishman Edward Bransfield or 3) American Nathaniel B. Palmer

First circumnavigation of Antarctica: By Fabian
von Bellingshausen from 1819–1821

First person to set foot on Antarctica: American
captain John Davis in 1821

First expedition to reach the South Pole:
Norway's Roald Amundsen, along with four colleagues and 52 sled dogs, on December 14, 1911. Britain's Robert Falcon Scott got there 35 days later, but he and his four companions died of cold and starvation on the return trip. The race between the two men captured the attention of the world and helped spur interest in Antarctic exploration.

First women to winter in Antarctica:
Edith Ronne and Jennie Darlington, who spent 1947 at East Base on Stonington Island as part of a 23-person expedition

First person to set foot on both
Poles: Dr. Albert Paddock Crary. He traveled to the North Pole by aircraft in 1952, and to the South Pole by tracked vehicle in 1961.

Africa

The continent of Africa may have been the home of the first human beings, according to many archaeologists. While it remained home to millions of people and animals, it was a mysterious place to European and, later, American explorers. Their "discoveries" helped open up Africa to the wider world, which didn't always work out too well for the Africans, because Europeans brought diseases and domination. Here are some momentous African exploration firsts:

First foreign colonies on the continent: Hanno,

a statesman in Carthage (Libya), founded six cities on the west coast of Africa in about 500 BCE.

First eyewitness account of life in the African interior by a European explorer: Alvise Ca' da

Mosto's *Book of the First Ocean Voyage to the Land of the Blacks of Lower Ethiopia*, published in 1507. Ca' da Mosto entered the Gambia River on the west coast of Africa and continued inland for 60 miles (96 km) in 1455. His book describes his adventures and the sights he saw.

First modern European to cross the Sahara:

German traveler Frederick Hornemann, who joined up with a caravan of African merchants in 1798

First Europeans to visit Mt. Kilimanjaro and Mt. Kenya: Johannes Rebmann and Ludwig Krapf of Germany in 1848

First European to find the source of the White Nile: Scottish explorer John Hanning Speke. In 1858 Speke reached Lake Victoria, the largest lake in Africa, and correctly identified it as the Nile's source.

First European to cross equatorial Africa from coast to coast: English naval officer Verney Cameron, who left Zanzibar in 1873 and arrived on the Angolan coast in 1875

"Dr. Livingstone, I presume?"

Scottish adventurer, medical missionary, and abolitionist David Livingstone was perhaps the most famous explorer of Africa. He was the first European to stumble upon the Zambezi River and Victoria Falls, both in 1855. In 1866, Livingstone set out to explore around Lake Albert; he disappeared for five years. It was a Welsh journalist, Henry M. Stanley, who set out to find Livingstone while on assignment for the *New York Herald*. He encountered the weakened Livingstone at Lake Tanganyika in 1871, addressing him with the famous line in this box's title. Stanley and Livingstone explored together for two years, until Livingstone died in Africa in 1873.

Asia of Old

The vast lands of Asia are filled with ancient cultures that have been there for thousands of years. But they were mostly cut off from Europe and other parts of the world until only about 600 years ago. Here are some key firsts in the history of European and Asian contacts:

Hello, India!

Portuguese navigator Vasco da Gama became the first European to sail to India, arriving in 1498. Earlier visitors had traveled over land.

Japan by Mistake

The first Europeans to visit Japan ended up there by accident. In 1543, several Portuguese traders were passengers on a Chinese ship that was wrecked off the coast of Japan. Coming ashore, they brought the first guns ever seen in Japan. They later returned to Europe with tales of this mysterious land.

Heading Into China

The first European to visit the court of the great Khans, rulers of China, was an Italian priest, Giovanni da Pian del Carpini, who arrived in 1246 after a 15-month journey. Marco Polo, the famous Italian adventurer, did not arrive until 1275.

Heading Out of China

In 1405, the emperor Zheng Hou led the first major expedition out of China over the sea. His vast fleet visited India, the Philippines, and even eastern Africa. One voyage returned with the first giraffe ever seen in China!

Down Under

You'd think that a place as big as Australia—the only island that's big enough to be its own continent!—wouldn't be hard to "discover." But for hundreds of years after Europeans first headed out on the waves of the world, Australia was still a mystery. Beginning in the 1600s, though, a series of explorers followed clues to solve it.

➤➤ The first European sighting of Australia (at least the first one that was written down) came in 1606. Dutch sailor Willem Jansz saw the island in the distance, but did not land.

➤➤ In 1616, Dutch merchant Dirk Hartog was sailing around the Spice Islands (in what is today the Philippines) when, well, he got lost. He saw in the distance some land and, as the saying goes, any port in a storm. He found that he had landed on what Jansz had first seen. Hartog was the first European to set foot on Australia.

➤➤ Spurred by those voyages and others by Dutch sailors (notably Abel Tasman), Captain James Cook of England sailed for Australia in the *Endeavour*. Landing there in 1770, he became the first to map the eastern coast of Australia. He also claimed the land for his king.

➤➤ In 1788, the "First Fleet" arrived from England with 11 ships full of the first European colonists in Australia.

➤➤ In 1803, Englishman Matthew Flinders became the first person to sail entirely around the enormous island continent of Australia. Flinders' circumnavigation meant that Australia was a mystery no longer.

Glub, Glub!

About 70 percent of Earth's surface is covered by seas and oceans, which means there's a lot of water out there to explore and create cool firsts. New submersible technology has made such discoveries more frequent in recent years, but no less dangerous. Here are some firsts from the world of the fishes:

First written account of diving: Japanese women dive to retrieve shellfish from the ocean floor, holding their breath for up to three minutes. Around 100 BCE.

First underwater studies of marine life: French zoologist Henri Milne-Edwards, off of Sicily in 1844

First underwater photograph: By William Thompson in 1856; he lowered a waterproof camera to a depth of 20 feet (6 m) in Weymouth Bay, England.

First underwater photos by a diver: Taken by Frenchman Louis Bouton in 1893

First exploration of Mariana Trench, deepest place in the world (35,800 feet; 10,912 m): Swiss oceanographer Jacques Piccard and U.S. Navy lieutenant Don Walsh reached the bottom of the trench in the bathyscaphe *Trieste* on January 23, 1960.

First national diver training organization: The Professional Association of Diving Instructors (PADI) was formed in 1966.

First photos taken of the wreck of the Titanic in the North Atlantic: 1985 by Robert Ballard's team

First Like a Fish

Former French naval officer Jacques-Yves Cousteau first dove underwater in 1935, wearing a pair of simple goggles. What he saw changed his life, and soon he would change the world of diving. In 1943, he became the first person to swim freely underwater using scuba gear, which he invented with the help of engineer Émile Gagnan. SCUBA actually stands for Self-Contained Underwater Breathing Apparatus. Scuba tanks and hoses supply divers with compressed air to let them breathe underwater. Cousteau also invented the regulator, a device that lets the diver breathe in oxygen and exhale carbon dioxide. As he continued to expand his explorations of the oceans, he became the host of the first regular TV show about the oceans, *The Undersea World of Jacques Cousteau*, which first aired in 1967. For nearly 50 years, Cousteau, who died in 1997, explored the depths of the world's oceans and rivers, adding to our understanding of undersea life.

Diving Gear Firsts

Exploring the undersea world means finding a way to breathe underwater. Cousteau's scuba gear made visiting relatively shallow depths possible. But inventors before and after him came up with other ways to visit the ocean depths:

First use of an underwater glass bell: Italians explored sunken ships in Lake Nemi in 1535 for an hour at a time, using a device invented by engineer Guglielmo de Lorena. A diver climbed into a large glass bell, which was then lowered into the water. Air pressure in the bell kept the water out of the top of the bell, giving the diver a pocket of air to breathe while looking around through the glass.

First diving suit: Englishman John Lethbridge built large cylinders, made from leather or wood, with armholes and glass panels for viewing; he took one down to 60 feet (18 m) in 1715.

First practical diving suit: After several inventors gave this "first" a shot, Leonard Norcross of Dixfield, Maine, created a version that worked consistently well. In 1834, he patented an airtight rubber "water-dress." A brass helmet was connected to an air pump by a rubber hose; the diver's foot coverings were weighted with lead to help him stay underwater.

First underwater breathing device: In 1865, French inventors Benoit Rouquayrol and Auguste Denayrouse created a steel tank that was strapped to a diver's back. A hose from the surface supplied the tank with air that the diver inhaled through a valve in his mouth.

First rubber goggles with glass lenses:
Guy Gilpatric invented them in 1930 to help divers see the underwater world more clearly.

First rubber foot fins: Invented in France in 1933 by Louis de Corlieu

First deep bathysphere trip: Naturalist William Beebe and designer Otis Barton descended in theirs to a record 3,028 feet (923 m) off Bermuda in 1934. Beebe had created several versions of this underwater craft. On this trip, they proved that it could descend safely to great depths. A bathysphere is an untethered craft that uses electric propellers to move around. Shaped like a ball or a sausage, it has a thick steel skin and chambers that fill with water to make it go up or down. In 1960, Jacques Piccard became the first person to descend more than 35,000 feet (10,668 m) under the ocean. That's more than six miles (10 km)!

Submarine Firsts

First test of a submarine: In England in 1620 by Dutch inventor Cornelis van Drebbel; it was a wooden craft powered by oarsmen.

First submarine used in combat: American David Bushnell's *Turtle* tried to place an explosive on a British ship in New York harbor in 1776. The trip was unsuccessful, but showed the potential of subs for military uses.

First atomic submarine: The *Nautilus*, launched January 21, 1954, from Groton, Connecticut

First sub to circle the globe without surfacing: The USS *Triton*, in 1960

Lewis and Clark

As America settled into nationhood in the early 1800s, many of its citizens looked west. In 1803, they had more to look at when Thomas Jefferson arranged the Louisiana Purchase, buying millions of acres of land from France. This land stretched from Louisiana north along the Missouri River to the Canadian border and west to the Pacific Ocean. Soon, the big question was, who would be the first to explore and map this huge new territory of the United States?

In 1803, Jefferson answered that question by choosing 29-year-old Meriwether Lewis, a U.S. Army captain and Jefferson's private secretary, to lead the first expedition. Lewis then picked William Clark, 33, his former Army superior, to join him. Both men had experience surviving in the wilderness and fighting Indians.

On May 14, 1804, Lewis and Clark took their first steps on the journey, leading about 50 men out of St. Louis and up the Missouri River. The expedition made its way up the Missouri to what is now North Dakota, then established its first winter camp, called Fort Mandan, near some peaceful Mandan Native American villages. Here they were joined by a French-Canadian trader, Toussaint Charbonneau; his Shoshone Indian wife, Sacagawea, who became the resident interpreter; and their baby.

Sacagawea's presence would soon become very valuable to the explorers. In August, they met a band of Shoshone whose chief was Sacagawea's brother. The Shoshone traded horses and supplies to the explorers and provided a guide to help them through the mountains. In November 1805, Lewis and Clark became the first Americans to reach the Pacific coast, stopping at what is now Astoria, Oregon. The expedition began the journey home the following spring, on March 23, 1806.

The United States soon claimed the Oregon region as its own as well, exciting the great pioneer rush of the mid-1800s. Lewis and Clark were the first Americans to see much of this land, and they created the first maps of the northwest United States. Virtually everything they did on their travels was a first, and their bravery and imagination helped create what western America is today.

The journals of Lewis and Clark, first published in a shortened version in 1814 and in their entirety in 1905, still make great reading.

Because They're There

The high peaks of the world's mountains have called to explorers for centuries. Becoming the first person to battle the elements to reach the peaks of various mountains has been a big goal for top climbers. Here are some stories about key firsts in mountaineering history:

First long written record of mountain climbing:
By Italian poet Francesco Petrarca in April 1336. After scaling 6,263-foot (1,909 m) Mount Ventoux in Provence, France, Petrarca wrote to an Augustinian monk, "I stood like one dazed. I beheld the clouds under our feet, and what I had read of [Greek mountains] Athos and Olympus seemed less incredible, as I myself witnessed the same things from a mountain less famous."

First mountaineer in the Alps:
Horace-Bénédict de Saussure, professor of physics and philosophy at the Academy of Geneva in Switzerland. Beginning in 1760, Saussure became the first "Alpine" climber when he made a series of groundbreaking climbs in the Swiss Alps.

First woman to reach the top of the highest mountain on every continent:
French climber Christine Janin, who completed the checklist by bagging Mt. Aconcagua in Argentina in 1992

First person to scale the highest mountains on all seven continents and visit both the North and South magnetic and geographic Poles on foot:

British explorer David Hempleman-Adams. The last destination was the geographic North Pole, which he nailed on April 28, 1998. Boy, he really got around!

Mount Everest
The World's Tallest Mountain

The north side of Mt. Everest is in Tibet, which was closed to outsiders for many years; the nation's spiritual leader, the Dalai Lama, opened the land in 1921. The Chinese took control of Tibet in 1950 and shut the borders, but Nepal let climbers approach Everest. New Zealander Edmund Hillary and Tenzing Norgay (a member of the local Sherpa community) were the first to reach the top, on May 29, 1953.

Other Everest firsts:

▲ The first American: James W. Whittaker, on May 1, 1963

▲ The first woman: Japanese climber Tabei Junko, deputy leader of an all-female expedition, in 1975—after surviving an avalanche that buried her under a giant block of ice!

▲ The first woman to climb solo: New Zealander Lydia Bradey, in 1988

▲ In 1998, Tom Whittaker, who lost a leg to a car accident, became the first disabled person to reach the top.

▲ The first blind climber to reach the top: American Erik Weihenmayer, in 2001

Going Up!

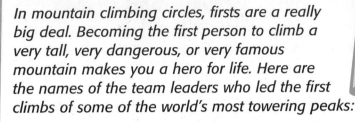

In mountain climbing circles, firsts are a really big deal. Becoming the first person to climb a very tall, very dangerous, or very famous mountain makes you a hero for life. Here are the names of the team leaders who led the first climbs of some of the world's most towering peaks:

MOUNTAIN (CONTINENT)	FIRST TO REACH TOP	YEAR
Mont Blanc (Europe)	Michel Paccard and Jacques Balmat	1786
Matterhorn (Europe)	Edward Whymper	1865
Rainier (N. America)	Hazard Stevens and P. B. Van Trump	1870
Elbrus* (Europe)	F. Crawford Grove	1874
Kilimanjaro* (Africa)	Hans Meyer	1889
Aconcagua* (S. America)	Matthias Zurbriggen	1897
Denali* (N. America)	Hudson Stuck, Harry P. Karstens	1913
K2 (Asia)	Ardito Desio	1954
Lhotse (Asia)	Ernst Reiss and Fritz Luchsinger	1956
Vinson Massif* (Antarctica)	Nicholas Clinch	1966

* Highest mountain on its continent

Mr. Mountain Firsts

Reinhold Messner is an Italian climber and adventurer who has collected these and other climbing firsts: *1978:* (with Peter Habeler) First ascent of Mount Everest without bottled oxygen. In the thin air of high altitude, most climbers must use oxygen bottles. *1980:* First solo ascent of Everest. *1982:* First climber to ascend the world's three tallest peaks: Everest in 1978, K2 in 1979, and Kanchenjunga in 1982. *1986:* First to climb the world's 14 tallest mountains (those higher than 26,250 feet or 8,000 m).

CHAPTER 5

Food

No one knows what people ate as the first food, but that doesn't mean we didn't come up with a whole plateful of food firsts! Wash your hands, get your napkin, and dig in! (And keep your elbows off the book!)

Food Beginnings

First, let's see where some foods came from . . . just not precisely when. Most of these are fruits and vegetables (you remember those, right?). The first food was whatever was growing wild. The earliest archaeological evidence of people growing food, including barley and wheat in the Middle East, dates to about 7000 BCE. Around the same time in Central America, people there were growing peppers and avocados. Here are some of the other food "first homes":

FOOD	PLACE FIRST GROWN	FOOD	PLACE FIRST GROWN
Apple	Southwestern Asia	**Maple syrup**	NE United States; SE Canada
Banana	Malaysia	**Olive**	Crete
Black pepper	India	**Peach**	China
Blueberry	North America	**Rice**	Southeast Asia
Broccoli	Southern Italy	**Spinach**	Persia
Corn	Mexico or Central America	**Tomato**	Mexico and Central America
Grapefruit	Jamaica		

Bonus:

You like cheese, right? Can't have a grilled cheese sandwich without it. No one knows who invented the ancient art of turning milk into cheese. But one of the most popular cheeses in the world was first made in 1666 in the village of Cheddar, England. One guess what cheese that is . . . and the answer is not "English."

Breakfast Time

Most of you wouldn't start your day without a healthy breakfast, right? Well, at least a big bowl of sugary cereal! For many years, though, most breakfast cereal, such as oatmeal, was served hot. Then in 1893, Will Kellogg and the Kellogg Company introduced the first popular cold cereal, Shredded Wheat. Here are some cereal firsts:

CEREAL	FIRST SOLD	CEREAL	FIRST SOLD
Corn Flakes	1894	Frosted Flakes	1952
Grape-Nuts	1897	Trix	1954
Wheaties	1921	Cocoa Puffs	1958
Rice Krispies	1929	Lucky Charms	1963
Cheerios	1941	Froot Loops	1963

A Ham Montagu?

Sandwiches are a handy and popular food made in thousands of ways. But sandwiches are not actually that old, as food goes. The first sandwich was created in 1762 when a hungry British politician named John Montagu, the Earl of Sandwich, refused to stop playing cards long enough to eat. He asked that meat and cheese be brought to him between slices of toast. The snack quickly caught on, taking part of Montagu's title as its name. Thanks, Earl!

Drink Up

If you guess that the first drink ever taken by people was water, then you're right. Heck, all those cavepeople had to do was open their mouths when it rained! Things have gotten much tastier for the thirsty people of the world since then. Here are some key firsts in the history of beverages, which is a fancy word for stuff you drink:

Tea and Coffee

First tea: No facts here, but a cool legend. According to the story, in 2727 BCE, Chinese emperor Shen Nong fell asleep under a tea tree. A leaf fell into his cup of water. He awoke, took a sip, and discovered something pretty tasty. The first book on tea was written in Chinese in 780 by an author named Lu Yu. Dutch traders brought the first tea from China to Europe in 1610. In 1657, tea was first sold in England by Thomas Garway.

First coffee drinking: The Galla people of Ethiopia chewed coffee beans as a stimulant, but it was the Arabs in about 1000 who learned to boil the beans and water into a drink.

First coffee with cream and sugar: Offered by Polish-born entrepreneur Franz George Kolshitsky at his coffeehouse (no, it was not a Starbucks) in Vienna, Austria, in 1683

First iced tea: Introduced at the Louisiana Purchase Exposition in St. Louis in 1904, by an Englishman named Richard Blechynden

First instant coffee: In 1901 in Chicago, Satori Kato came up with the first way to mix coffee grounds with water to make—ta-dah!—instant coffee!

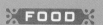

Pop Goes the World

Whether you say soda or pop or just "Gimmee!," flavored, sugary, carbonated beverages are among the world's most popular drinks. They were first sold in glass bottles. Soft-drink cans came along in 1960, and pop-tops (the old removable kind) were first used in 1963. Here are some soda firsts:

DRINK	FIRST SOLD	INVENTOR
First ginger ale	1850	Cantrell & Cochrane Co., Ireland
First Dr Pepper	1884	R. S. Lazenby, Texas
First Coca-Cola	1886	John S. Pemberton, Georgia
First Pepsi-Cola	1898	Caleb Bradham, North Carolina
First diet soda, No-Cal	1952	Hyman Kirsch, New York
First Diet Coke	1981	Coca-Cola Co., Georgia

What's Your Vote?

As it turned out, 1927 was quite a year for popular beverages. On April 8 of that year, Ottawa's Laurentian Dairy introduced homogenized milk, in which the fat is broken up and dissolved into the liquid. Otherwise, milk separates naturally into two parts, one thin and watery, the other squishy and lumpy. That same year, inventor Edwin E. Perkins of Nebraska introduced Kool-Aid. Parents probably would choose the new milk as the most significant development of '27; kids probably would vote for the Kool-Aid.

Zapped! A New Wave

During World War II, British and American scientists used magnetrons—which are long tubes that produce a kind of energy called microwaves—while they were inventing radar. An accidental discovery in 1946 led to the first microwave oven.

Dr. Percy Spencer, an eighth-grade dropout and electronics whiz, was an engineer with the Raytheon Manufacturing Corporation. He was testing a magnetron tube at the company's lab in Waltham, Massachusetts, one day when he reached into his pocket for a candy bar. To his surprise, Spencer found a gooey mess where his solid chocolate used to be.

# of Food Appears

He knew that microwaves generated heat, but he hadn't felt any heat coming from the magnetron. Had the magnetron melted his candy? To test a hunch, Spencer got a bag of popcorn kernels and set them near the tube. Within minutes the kernels were popping all over the lab.

The next morning, Spencer brought a dozen eggs to work. He cut a hole in a pot, put an egg inside, and aligned the hole with the beam of the magnetron. The egg soon exploded. It had cooked from the inside out. Spencer filed a patent for a device that he said "cooked food faster and more efficiently than any conventional cooker."

By 1947, Raytheon had manufactured the first microwave oven, called the Radarange. It was as big as a refrigerator, though the cooking compartment was about the same size as a modern microwave oven. Raytheon sold only a few Radaranges, mostly for use in restaurants and on trains.

In 1952, the Tappan Company offered the first microwave oven for home use. It featured an on-off switch, two cooking speeds, and a 21-minute timer. It retailed for a staggering $1,295! Many models cost less than $100 today. Over the next 20 years, Spencer's chocolate-melting tube turned into an appliance that is a regular part of American kitchens.

Snack Attack

What would life be like without snacks? We're afraid to think about it. But as much as snack food is a big part of your diet (not too big, we hope), it all had to start somewhere. Here are some snackin' firsts:

First popcorn: This crunchy snack was probably first grown by Native Americans around 3000 BCE.

First pretzels: In Italy in the year 610, parents created these treats to give to children who had learned their prayers.

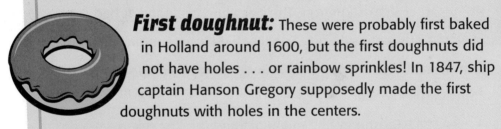

First doughnut: These were probably first baked in Holland around 1600, but the first doughnuts did not have holes . . . or rainbow sprinkles! In 1847, ship captain Hanson Gregory supposedly made the first doughnuts with holes in the centers.

First Graham cracker: Sylvester Graham, a minister and vegetarian, created these brownish crackers in 1829 to encourage people to eat a fiber-rich type of wheat flour.

First potato chips: Thin potato slices first met boiling oil in Saratoga Springs, New York, in 1853. The result was snack history!

First yogurt sold commercially: Yogurt is an ancient food, dating back many thousands of years. Records of the Mongol conqueror Genghis Khan from the 1200s show that his armies ate tons of yogurt. But it was not until 1908 in Russia that yogurt was produced commercially and sold in stores.

First Cracker Jack: Invented by German immigrant Frederick William Rueckheim, it first appeared at the Chicago World's Fair in 1893. Cracker Jack began adding small metal (later plastic or paper) toys to each package in 1912.

First Girl Scout cookies: The drive to raise money for the troops—and thrill fans of Thin Mints!—was first held in 1922.

First peanut butter: The sticky stuff was first ground in 1890 by a St. Louis company owned by George Bayles. At the 1904 World's Fair, C. H. Sumner was the first to sell peanut butter on a wide scale. The famous Skippy peanut butter was introduced by Rosefield Packing Co. of California in 1932.

First Fig Newtons: In 1891, these cookies were first produced by the Kennedy Biscuit Works, a company later called Nabisco, with a machine invented by James Henry Mitchell.

First Jell-O: Pearl Wait and his wife, May, who came up with the name, made the first Jell-O in 1897, but it was not available for sale until 1902.

First Velveeta cheese: Processed cheese was invented in 1928, with the introduction of Velveeta by Kraft.

First Fritos: The first corn chips hit the snack rack in 1932 when Fritos were first sold by San Antonio, Texas, candymaker C. Elmer Doolin.

First Lunchables: Lunch and a snack together? What will they think of next? These were first sold by the Oscar Mayer company in 1988.

This Page Is

Sweet tooths of the world, unite! Without candy . . . well, we don't like to think of a world without candy. But once upon a time, candy bars were unheard of, and gum was not around to be chewed. Fortunately for us, a lot of smart people did a lot of tasty things with sugar, chocolate, nuts, and other good stuff. So here are some highlights from the history of candy:

First chocolate in Europe (1520): Chocolate was part of several ancient cultures in Central and South America, but Europeans didn't discover it until explorer Hernán Cortés went back to Spain. Then the Spaniards kept it a secret from the rest of Europe for almost a century!

First known candy canes (1670): The choirmaster (whose name is lost to history) at Cologne Cathedral in Germany bent sugar sticks into canes to represent a shepherd's staff and hung them on the church Christmas tree. The all-white candy canes were handed out to children during the long holiday church services. The exact inventor of the red-and-white striped version is unknown, but in 1900, Christmas card illustrations showed for the first time that pattern so familiar to kids today.

First modern chocolate bar (1847): In England, Joseph Fry & Son discovered a way to mix chocolate with nuts, caramels, jellies, and other sweet treats so that it could be molded into a handy shape.

First boxes of chocolate candies (1868): Candymaker John Cadbury (yep, that Cadbury) of England created chocolates in a variety of fun shapes, put them together in a box, and invented something that we can give our moms on Mother's Day!

NOT for Dentists

First appearance of cotton candy (1900): Ringling Brothers Circus shows started selling the sticky stuff after Thomas Patton made the first cotton candy–making machine.

First LifeSavers (1912): Named for the circular rings carried on ships, they were introduced by Cleveland chocolate manufacturer Clarence Crane. The first flavor? Peppermint.

First Marshmallow Peeps (1953): You know those little yellow or pink chicks sold in the spring? They were first sold by the Just Born company of Bethlehem, Pennsylvania.

Gumming Up the World

1848 John B. Curtis made and sold the first chewing gum, State of Maine Pure Spruce Gum.

1871 The first nationally successful brand of chewing gum was Black Jack, made by Thomas Adams.

1888 Tutti-Frutti gum, made by Charles Adams, became the first to be sold in a vending machine (in a New York City subway station).

1906 Frank Fleer invented the first bubble gum, called Blibber-Blubber. It was never sold.

1928 One of Fleer's employees, Walter Diemer, came up with the successful Double Bubble, a pink bubble gum.

Eating Out

Raise your hand if you or your parents have eaten at a restaurant or even brought home takeout food in the past week. Did you know that a few hundred years ago, almost no one had done that even once? There were, of course, many inns or taverns that sold food to the public, but they were not like restaurants of today. Here are some key firsts in the history of restaurants and dining out:

The **first place to be called a restaurant** was opened in Paris, France, in 1765, by a man named Boulanger. He served soups and broths, which he called *restaurants*, or "restoratives." The idea caught on, and by 1804 Paris boasted more than 500 similar dining establishments.

America's first restaurant was opened in Boston in 1794 by a Frenchman, Jean-Baptiste Gilbert Payplat. Many bars or inns were already around, of course, but none offered the services of a true restaurant.

SAY IT FIRST...

first course Also known as an "appetizer" or an "hors d'oeuvre," a first course is a small portion of food served before the main part of a meal. It is intended to taste good and stimulate the appetite without filling you up. Some popular first courses are chips and salsa, green salad, and soup.

Most food historians agree the ***first American cafeteria*** (a place where all the food is laid out for people to choose from) opened in 1891 at the YWCA of Kansas City, Missouri.

New York City is full of places to buy great pizza. Lombardi's, the ***first pizzeria*** there, opened in 1895.

The ***first drive-through restaurant*** opened in Glendale, California, in 1936.

The ***first revolving restaurant*** opened in 1956. It is located atop a 700-foot (213-m) tower in Stuttgart, Germany.

McFirsts

Kids in Downey, California, probably didn't know it at the time, but in 1954 they were present at the creation of the biggest restaurant chain in the world.

By that time, brothers Mac and Dick McDonald owned several small hamburger stands. An enthusiastic young milk-shake machine salesman named Ray Kroc got permission to open a branch of McDonald's in Downey. The stand he opened in 1954 is still operating today. Ray opened another in Des Plaines, Illinois, in 1955. By 1961, Ray owned the entire company and set about building a booming eating empire that now spans the world. Here are some fun first facts about a place probably every one of you has been to at least once!

1963 Ronald McDonald first appeared.

1964 The Filet-o-Fish made its debut.

1967 First McDonald's opened outside the U.S., in Canada.

1968 The Big Mac made its first appearance.

1971 In Chula Vista, California, kids played at the first McDonald's PlayLand.

1972 The Quarter-Pounder arrived.

1973 Egg McMuffin was first served.

1975 The first McDonald's drive-through opened in Arizona.

1983 Chicken McNuggets were born!

1990 McDonald's opened in Moscow.

1992 First McDonald's in China opened in Beijing.

More Fast Food

Of course, Mickey D's is not the only fast-food place in the world. Here are years and places that a whole bunch of other fast-food places opened:

RESTAURANT	PLACE	FIRST YEAR
White Castle	Wichita, Kansas	1921
Krispy Kreme	Winston-Salem, N. Carolina	1937
Dairy Queen	Joliet, Illinois	1940
Carl's Jr.	Anaheim, California	1945
Dunkin' Donuts	Quincy, Massachusetts	1950
Jack in the Box	San Diego, California	1951
Kentucky Fried Chicken	Salt Lake City, Utah	1952
Burger King	Miami, Florida	1954
Pizza Hut	Kansas City, Missouri	1958
Little Caesars	Garden City, Michigan	1959
Hardee's	Greenville, N. Carolina	1960
Taco Bell	Downey, California	1962
Domino's	Ypsilanti, Michigan	1965
Subway	Bridgeport, Connecticut	1965
Wendy's	Columbus, Ohio	1969
Quiznos	Denver, Colorado	1981

American Pie

Some of the world's best and most famous kinds of food were born in the United States. You might not have tried all of these, but together, they make a mighty nice menu.

First Hot Dog

Sausage in a bun, of course!

Sausage has been around for centuries and sold on city streets all over America. However, the first sausage on a bun to be called a hot dog was sold at the Chicago World's Fair in 1893.

First Eggs Benedict

Poached eggs and creamy yellow hollandaise sauce on top of an English muffin

Legend has it a Wall Street banker named Benedict asked the chef at Delmonico's restaurant in Manhattan to whip up something new in the 1920s. This dish is what he came up with.

First French Dip Sandwich

Roast beef sandwich served with a cup of beef juice for dipping

In 1918, Philippe Mathieu was making a sandwich for a policeman at his restaurant, Philippe the Original in Los Angeles. Mathieu accidentally dropped the French roll into the drippings of a pan, and the officer loved it. A sandwich tradition was born!

First Buffalo Wings

Small chicken wings served in very spicy sauce

There are some arguments about who really came up with this popular and handy food. The most often-told version is that they

were first sold in 1964 by Teressa Bellissimo of the Anchor Bar & Restaurant in Buffalo, New York.

First Caesar Salad

Lettuce salad with an oil, egg, and anchovy dressing

Okay, so it wasn't exactly America, but Caesar Cardini was right across the border in Tijuana, Mexico, when he created this popular salad in 1924.

First Pie à la Mode

Pie, usually apple pie, with a scoop of vanilla ice cream on top

After frequent meals at the Cambridge Hotel in Washington County, New York, in the 1890s, Charles Watson Townsend often ordered ice cream with his apple pie. Fellow diner Mrs. Berry Hall coined the name.

First Po'boy Sandwich

French bread loaf split in half and filled with a variety of ingredients, such as ham, beef, cheese, or oysters

Popular in New Orleans and around the South, it was created in the 1920s by store owners Benny and Clovis Martin, who served the sandwich to striking streetcar workers in New Orleans. The name comes from the Martins' worry about the workers, whom they called "poor boys." (There are other stories about the invention of this food, but this is the most carefully documented.)

First Philly Cheesesteak

Thinly sliced steak grilled with onions, served on a roll with cheese

Pat Olivieri sold sandwiches in South Philadelphia before World War II. In 1930, he made himself a new kind of sandwich for lunch that soon became the city's signature dish.

Brrrr! Cold Stuff

Ice Cream, You Scream

First written recipe for ice cream: Around the year 15 by Roman general Quintus Maximus, who was nicknamed "The Glutton" (a person who eats waaay too much food)

First modern-style ice cream: Made in Florence, Italy, in 1565

First ice-cream parlor: Opened in Paris in 1670 by a Sicilian, Francisco Procopio

First hand-cranked ice-cream maker: Invented by American Nancy Johnson in 1846

First modern ice-cream factory: Built by Jacob Fussell, a Baltimore milk dealer, in 1851

First ice-cream cone: Sold at the Louisiana Purchase Exposition in St. Louis in 1904; a waffle was twisted into a cone shape and filled with ice cream.

First Eskimo Pie: Made in 1919 in an Iowa sweetshop

The Improbable Popsicle

In 1923, Oakland, California, lemonade-mix salesman Frank Epperson accidentally left a glass of lemonade on his windowsill overnight. He woke in the morning to find it frozen, with the spoon handle sticking out of the glass. Instead of just thawing it out, he realized he had a new tasty treat on his hands. Well, on his windowsill at least. He applied for a patent, and a year later was granted one for the "Epsicle." He soon marketed the wonder as a Popsicle.

First Frozen Foods

The first frozen food was probably made when a caveman kept some leftover sabertooth tiger meat outside the cave overnight. But that was too chancy. The key to frozen food was being able to freeze it quickly so that it remained fresh. Another key was to have the foods taste the same after they were unfrozen. In 1923, Clarence Birdseye invented a quick-freezing method that solved both  those problems for the first time. The first frozen foods sold to the public were put on the market in 1930.

Supermarket Firsts

Get out your shopping lists; it's time to go to the market. One of the first places you'd go to find food is a supermarket. So let's find out some food-shopping firsts:

➡ The first known marketplace in the American colonies (the grandparent of the supermarket?) was established in Boston by order of Governor John Winthrop in 1634.

➡ So there were markets—but how do we get the groceries home? All sorts of boxes and bags, of course, but the first flat-bottomed brown-paper grocery bag was the Stillwell paper bag, patented in 1872.

➡ The first cash register was invented by James Ritty and patented by him and John Birch in 1883.

➡ America's first self-service stores opened in Pomona and Ocean Park, California, in 1912. Previously, large markets had not let customers pick out their own food.

➡ The first American supermarket chain was the Piggly Wiggly market. It first opened in 1916 in Memphis, Tennessee.

➡ A Piggly Wiggly owner in Oklahoma City named Sylvan Goldman made the first grocery cart in 1937. It was made from a folding chair with an attached basket.

➨ The first bar code technology was patented way back in 1952 by Bernard Silver and Norman Joseph Woodland of Drexel Institute of Technology in Philadelphia, Pennsylvania. A special printing process created a series of lines that could be read by a special machine. In 1974, at a Marsh's market in Troy, Ohio, a 10-pack of Wrigley's gum became the first item to have its bar code scanned at a checkout counter.

MY FIRST...

The first time I cooked a meal all by myself,

I was _____ years old.

I chose to make _____

_____.

This is who ate it: _____

_____.

The hardest thing about making it was _____

_____.

The fun part was _____

_____.

_____ cleaned up the mess afterward.

People said the food was _____

_____.

Kitchen Gear

Food doesn't just cook itself. Chefs (and your mom and dad!) need lots of tools and implements to make the dishes you love to eat. Here are some firsts from the world of the kitchen drawers:

First patented can opener:

1858, by Ezra J. Warner of

Waterbury, Connecticut

Readin' Recipes

Believe it or not, your parents have not memorized all the recipes they use for making you cakes, cookies, and those veggies you enjoy so much. They sometimes use cookbooks.

First known cookbook: *Hedypatheia* (Pleasant Living), by Greek author Archestratus about 350 BCE

First cookbook in English: *The Forme of Cury [Curry]*, compiled in England circa 1390; nobody knows who wrote it.

First printed cookbook: *De Honeste Voluptate ac Caletudine* (*Concerning Honest Pleasure and Well-Being*), by Italian Bartolema Scappi in 1485. It mainly consisted of desserts.

First cookbook written for homemakers: Probably Elizabeth Acton's *Modern Cookery for Private Families*, published in London in 1845

First electric can opener: 1931

First American restaurant to offer forks to its customers: The City Tavern in Philadelphia, around the 1740s. Before that, customers just used their hands! No, just kidding, they used spoons and knives. Forks were a more recent innovation.

First stainless-steel tableware: Knives manufactured in 1921 at the Silver Company of Meriden, Connecticut

First made-in-America cooking utensil: The Saugus Pot, a one-quart-capacity, cast-iron pot produced at the Saugus Iron Works in the old Massachusetts colony city of Lynn in 1642

First enameled cookware: 1788, produced by the Konigsbronn foundry in Wurttemberg, Germany

First S.O.S. scouring pads: 1917, invented by door-to-door cookware salesman Edwin W. Cox in San Francisco. Cox offered the pads as free giveaways, and they soon outsold his pots and pans.

First whistling teakettle: 1921, devised by retired cookware executive Joseph Block and manufactured by a teakettle factory in Westphalia, Germany

Get It to Go!

We can't eat all our meals around the family table. We also can't sit down for a nice restaurant meal every day. Sometimes, you just have to eat and run. Here are some of the firsts from the world of portable food:

First canned food: The French Emperor Napoleon offered a prize of 12,000 francs (equivalent to nearly $400,000 today) to anyone who could devise a way to preserve food in airtight containers. Parisian candymaker Nicolas Appert, using jars and bottles, claimed the prize in 1809, packing soups, preserves, and vegetables. Oddly, the can opener was not invented until 1858 (see page 136). Until then they used hammers, nails, spikes, or axes. Really!

First Thermos bottle for home use: Patented in 1903 by German glassblower Reinhold Burger

First paper cups: 1908 in London, in response to sickness spread by germs. People could buy a clean paper cup of water from a machine.

First aluminum foil: 1947, produced by Richard S. Reynolds of the U.S. Foil Co. This handy, flexible stuff found a thousand uses in the home, such as keeping food fresh.

First Tupperware: Made by chemist Earl Tupper in 1948. That's right . . . thanks to Earl, we have leftovers.

First milk cartons: Invented in 1951 by Ruben Rausing of Sweden. Before that, milk came in glass bottles.

First juice boxes: Swedish scientists invented this "aseptic packaging" used to make juice boxes in the late 1970s (aseptic means germ-free). Now you can brag that you know the real name for those boxes.

CHAPTER 6

Government

Who makes the laws? Who are the head honchos? Who keeps the peace? More importantly, as far as we're concerned . . . who did all that first?! Read on to find out!

We the People

John

U.S. Firsts

American history is full of firsts. We started a country from scratch in 1776, so the government set a new first with nearly all of its officers in those early years. Here are some of the key first people in our government:

OFFICE (YEAR)	FIRST OFFICEHOLDER
President (1789)	*George Washington**
Vice President (1789)	*John Adams*
Cabinet officer/Treasury (1789)	*Alexander Hamilton*
Attorney General (1789)	*Edmund Randolph*
Speaker of the House (1789)	*Frederick Muhlenberg*
President Pro Tempore # (1789)	*John Langdon*
Chief Justice of the Supreme Court (1789)	*John Jay*
Secretary of State (1790)	*Thomas Jefferson*

* See page 142 for more!   # A key officer of the Senate

Other Firsts

☆ In 1781, Thomas McKean of Delaware was called the first "President of the United States in Congress Assembled." He was named that by the Continental Congress, which preceded the establishment of the United States Congress.

☆ The House of Representatives first met on March 4, 1789, in New York City.

☆ The U.S. Senate first convened on the same day.

☆ The first "First Lady" (the president's wife) was Martha Washington.

The First States

Here are the dates that the first 13 colonies became states:

STATE	DATE
Delaware	Dec. 7, 1787
Pennsylvania	Dec. 12, 1787
New Jersey	Dec. 18, 1787
Georgia	Jan. 2, 1788
Connecticut	Jan. 9, 1788
Massachusetts	Feb. 6, 1788
Maryland	April 28, 1788
South Carolina	May 23, 1788
New Hampshire	June 21, 1788
Virginia	June 25, 1788
New York	July 26, 1788
North Carolina	Nov. 21, 1789
Rhode Island	May 29, 1790

IN THE FIRST PLACE...

George Washington

A t the funeral for George Washington in 1799, General Henry "Light-Horse Harry" Lee said Washington was "first in war, first in peace, and first in the hearts of his countrymen." The Virginia planter-turned-soldier proved his leadership skill during the American Revolution and the postwar efforts to build a new nation. Few people could have imagined anyone else but Washington as the first U.S. president.

Washington was not the smartest leader of the revolutionary era. And some military officers questioned his battlefield tactics. Yet Washington commanded respect. He fought bravely and inspired confidence in the people around him. He also believed he and other Americans had a duty to serve the greater public good, instead of seeking personal gain.

Washington's military career began in 1753. The next year, he led a group of soldiers against a small force of French scouts. The battle marked the start of the French and Indian War. During the American Revolution, he served as commander in chief of the Continental Army. Washington overcame frequent shortages of men and supplies to lead the Americans to victory.

In 1787, Washington was chosen as the president of the Constitutional Convention. He supported the strong national government created by the Constitution and easily won the first presidential election held under it in 1789. He then helped define the position for the presidents who followed him. Washington asserted the president's right to conduct foreign policy, limiting Congress's influence. He also added the last words now spoken by all presidents as they take the oath of office: ". . . so help me

God." Most importantly, Washington helped Americans trust the new Constitution, the U.S. government, and the presidency itself.

Many books have been written about Washington's roles as general and president. And these Web sites have information on the man called the Father of His Country:

• The Papers of George Washington, http://gwpapers.virginia.edu/
• The President of the United States (POTUS) page on Washington, http://www.ipl.org/div/potus/gwashington.html

Presidential Firsts

George Washington gets all the glory because he was elected as the first president. But there have been 42 presidents since him, and many of them have notched firsts of their own. Here are a few of the most interesting or unusual:

First president to . . .

. . . shake hands instead of bow when meeting people: Thomas Jefferson

. . . wear pants instead of knee breeches: James Madison

. . . name his son after George Washington: John Quincy Adams

. . . ride on a train: Andrew Jackson

. . . be born in the United States: Martin Van Buren

. . . be unmarried when elected: James Buchanan

. . . have a telephone in the White House: Rutherford B. Hayes

. . . wear a beard while in office: Abraham Lincoln

. . . use electricity in the White House: Benjamin Harrison

. . . ride in a car: Theodore Roosevelt

... receive the Nobel Peace Prize: Theodore Roosevelt

... throw out the first ball at a baseball game: William Taft

... travel underwater in a submarine: Harry Truman

... have been a Boy Scout: John Kennedy

... resign from office: Richard Nixon

... be appointed instead of elected: Gerald Ford

... be born in a hospital: Jimmy Carter

... appoint a woman to the Supreme Court: Ronald Reagan

... have been a Rhodes Scholar: Bill Clinton

... have once owned a baseball team: George W. Bush

Vice Firsts

Why let presidents get all the fun? Here are some vice presidential firsts:

➺ First to succeed to the presidency after the death of the president: John Tyler became president in 1841 after the death of William Henry Harrison.

➺ First Native-American vice president: Charles Curtis (1929–1933), whose ancestors were part of the Osage tribe

➺ First woman nominated by a major party to run for vice president: Geraldine Ferraro (Democrat), who ran unsuccessfully with Walter Mondale in 1984

First Words

America and other nations are built on documents made up of words that express ideals. These documents spell out how a nation is formed or how it is governed. Here are the first sentences, just as they were originally written and spelled, of three of the most important documents in American history:

Declaration of Independence (1776)

When in the Course of human events, it becomes necessary for one people to dissolve the political bands which have connected them with another, and to assume among the powers of the earth, the separate and equal station to which the Laws of Nature and of

Nature's God entitle them, a decent respect to the opinions of mankind requires that they should declare the causes which impel them to the separation.

(As you probably know, John Hancock of Massachusetts was the first person to sign the Declaration of Independence.)

SAY IT FIRST...

First Amendment rights

The First Amendment of the Bill of Rights of the Constitution spells out some of the most important rights given to all Americans: freedom of religion, speech, and the press, plus freedom to gather peacefully. Together, they are called our First Amendment rights.

Constitution (1787)

We the People of the United States, in order to form a more perfect Union, establish Justice, insure domestic Tranquility, provide for the common defence, promote the general Welfare, and secure the Blessings of Liberty to ourselves and our Posterity, do ordain and establish this Constitution for the United States of America.

Bill of Rights (1791)

Amendment 1: Congress shall make no law respecting an establishment of religion, or prohibiting the free exercise thereof; or abridging the freedom of speech, or of the press; or the right of the people peaceably to assemble, and to petition the Government for a redress of grievances.

Elections and Parties

Through elections, Americans (and people in many other nations) choose the people to lead them. In America, the elections usually involve people from the Democratic and Republican Parties (though there are lots of smaller parties). Here are some firsts about American elections or political parties:

1789 First presidential election

1804 First election to choose vice presidents separately. Prior to this election, the vice president was the person who had received the second-most votes. Beginning in 1804, the vice president was nominated and the position was voted on as a separate office.

1824 First election decided by the House of Representatives. None of the candidates received a majority of the votes cast. In that case, under the rules of the day, Representatives voted on who would be the president. John Quincy Adams won that vote and became president.

May 21, 1832 First Democratic Party national convention

November 7, 1848 First day on which all Americans voted for president on the same day

February 22, 1854 First Republican Party convention. Political parties now hold conventions during presidential election years to decide their candidates. Oddly, the party known today as the Democrats was first called the Democratic-Republicans. In 1840, they dropped the Republican part.

1924 First political convention broadcast on radio was the 1924 Republican convention from Cleveland

1940 First convention to be televised was the 1940 Democratic convention in Philadelphia

1952 First election in which a computer predicted the result. The computer correctly picked Dwight Eisenhower as the winner over Adlai Stevenson only an hour after the final voting was over.

September 26, 1960 First presidential debates on TV. This was the first of four debates between Vice President Richard Nixon and Senator John Kennedy; Kennedy later won the election.

1997 First American to vote from space. Astronaut John Blaha received special permission from the state of Texas to cast his vote in a state election via a coded e-mail sent from orbit around Earth.

Military Firsts

Keeping America safe and secure is the important job of the nation's military forces. The army, navy, air force, marines, and coast guard are the five main parts of the American military. Here are some firsts from their long and distinguished histories:

First general of the Continental army: George Washington, 1775

First U.S. Navy fleet: 1775, authorized by Continental Congress

First coast guard service: Revenue Cutter Service, 1790; it became the U.S. Coast Guard in 1915.

First American military draft: 1792

First Marine band: 1798

First military balloons: In 1861, during the Civil War, balloons floated over battlefields and sent back reports.

First Navy admiral: David Farragut, 1866

First U.S. military airplane division: Established as part of the Signal Corps in 1914

SAY IT FIRST...

first lieutenant A military rank used in the U.S. Army. A lieutenant ranks above a sergeant and below a major. Other "first" ranks are first sergeant (U.S. Army) and petty officer first class (U.S. Navy and U.S. Coast Guard).

A Mighty Medal

Military feats are honored with medals, also called decorations. The first medal created for American servicepeople was the Medal of Merit (now known as the Purple Heart), first given out in 1782 by Gen. George Washington. Here are some firsts from the history of the highest award given to American servicepeople—the Congressional Medal of Honor:

⚙ First recipient: Pvt. Jacob Parrott, 1862

⚙ First African-American recipient: William Carney, 1863

⚙ First (and still only) female recipient: Mary Walker, 1865

⚙ First Hispanic recipient: David Barkley, 1918

⚙ First Native-American recipient: Ernest Childers, 1943

⚙ First Asian-American recipients: 22 soldiers, 2000*

*In 2000, President Bill Clinton awarded 22 Asian-American former soliders with the MOH for actions they undertook during World War II. Army policies in those days did not permit Japanese Americans and others from receiving such medals. Congress corrected this mistake more than 50 years later.

First army serial number: ASN-1, given to Sgt. Arthur Crean in 1918. Since then, all members of the military have received an identification number. Each serviceperson gets a unique number.

First army jeep: Built in 1940

First parachute unit: 1940

First female army unit: Women's Army Auxiliary Corps, 1942

First five-star generals: Hap Arnold, Dwight Eisenhower, Douglas MacArthur, and George Marshall were all raised to that rank on the same day in 1944.

Police Procedures

America boasts thousands of outstanding men and women who help make our society run smoothly. But police departments had to start somewhere. Here are some firsts for the folks wearing snappy blue uniforms in our cities and towns:

In 1631, citizens of Boston organized the **first "night watch."** Volunteers patrolled the streets watching for trouble.

The **first police force in America** was made up of eight men in New Amsterdam (now New York City), in 1658.

The **first state police** were the Texas Rangers, created in 1823 even though Texas was then a part of the nation of Mexico.

The **first police force** aimed at preventing crime was formed in 1845 in New York City, modeled after the London, England, force established in 1829.

The Boston Police Department bought the **first police car** in 1903. In 1904, New York City started the **first police motorcycle squad**. (In 1899, the Akron, Ohio, force had tried out an electric wagon.)

Cops on Bikes!

Police started their work on foot, then jumped on horseback. They added cars and motorcycles when those vehicles came along. But in 1987, Seattle, Washington, became the first city in America to have some of its police officers use bicycles! Seattle police helped create specially equipped mountain bikes. Officers began using them in the busy downtown area. Soon many other cities discovered that this was a handy and efficient type of police patrol. Plus, the officers stay in top shape from riding around all day!

The St. Louis, Missouri, police were the **first to use fingerprinting** as an official part of their identification system.

The **first woman to be a police officer** with full powers was Alice Wells in Los Angeles in 1910. In 1893, Marie Owen, a patrolman's widow, was named to the Detroit police, but in more of an honorary job. The first female police detective was Isabella Goodwin of New York City, who got her gold shield in 1912.

Dolly Spencer was the **first woman police chief**, named to lead the Milford, Ohio, force in 1914. In 1985, Penny Harrington of Portland, Oregon, was the first female chief of a major city police force.

Fire Dept. Firsts

The first fire departments were in ancient Rome. Called "vigiles," they used bronze water pumps to extinguish blazes. It was not until 1518 that the first mobile fire pumps were built on carts. The city of Augsburg, Germany, boasted the first. The flexible fire hose (made of leather) was invented by Jan van der Heijden of the Netherlands in 1672. Many early fire departments were run by fire insurance companies. They would work to save buildings that had bought insurance, while letting others burn! From the world of bravery, here are other firefighting firsts:

1654 America's first fire engine rolled onto the streets of Lynn, Massachusetts. Joseph Jencks created it out of a wooden barrel with iron wheels and pumps.

1659 Peter Stuyvesant, governor of New Amsterdam (later New York City), distributed leather buckets, ladders, and hooks to use in putting out fires. He also started an alarm system made up of rattles.

1679 America's first official fire department staffed by paid firefighters was formed in Boston, Massachusetts.

1800 New York City put the first fireboats into action. They were operated by 12 oarsmen and had a hand pump to pull water from the river or harbor.

1801 The first fire hydrant in America was installed in Philadelphia.

1852 Alexander Latta of Cincinnati made the first practical and successful fire engine. A steam engine ran the pump that shot out the water, and the whole rig was pulled by four horses.

1878 Engine Co. No. 21 of New York City boasted the first firehouse pole, so that firefighters could quickly get from their upstairs quarters to their gear below.

1937 For the first time, residents of London could call a simple emergency number to report a fire; they dialed 999.

1943 Due to World War II, all the firefighters in Ashville, New York, were called to the military. This led to the first all-female fire department, served by 13 women.

1947 For the first time, helicopters were used in fighting fires, dropping water on forest blazes in California. In 1955, an airplane designed for dropping water and chemicals on fires was first used on a fire in the Mendocino National Forest in California.

1968 The 911 emergency call system was put into operation in the United States for the first time.

More U.S. Firsts

Here's a hodgepodge of firsts from American history:

☛ The bald eagle first became the official symbol of the United States in 1782. Benjamin Franklin, as you trivia buffs know, had suggested the turkey instead.

☛ The first state admitted to the Union after the original 13 colonies was Vermont, which joined in 1791.

☛ The first (and only) state denied admission to the Union was the proposed state of Franklin. Its citizens had broken away from the rest of North Carolina in 1784.

☛ South Carolina became the first state to break away from the Union before the Civil War on December 20, 1860.

☛ The country's name was first approved in 1776, when United States was picked over United Colonies.

Flag Firsts

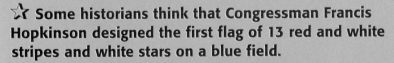

☆ On June 14, 1777, Congress officially made the "Stars and Stripes" the flag of the United States.

☆ Some historians think that Congressman Francis Hopkinson designed the first flag of 13 red and white stripes and white stars on a blue field.

☆ Legends—but few historians—tell that Betsy Ross of Philadelphia sewed the first flag.

☆ In 1831, ship captain William Driver was the first to call the flag "Old Glory."

CHAPTER 7

Grab Bag

This chapter is like the junk drawer in your room. You know, where you keep all that little stuff that doesn't seem to fit anywhere else. That's what we've got in here (except without all the dust)—firsts from the worlds of animals, buildings, roller coasters, dinosaurs, and more!

Animal Kingdom

Animals are all around us . . . heck, just look in a mirror! On these pages, read some animal firsts, from canine movie stars to flying cats to America's first zoo. This would be a good page, by the way, to read to your pets.

First horses in the New World were brought by Spanish explorer Hernan Cortes in 1519.

First cattle to be brought to the American colonies arrived at Plymouth Colony in 1624 from England. The first sheep had come over 15 years earlier.

First animal rights group, American Society for the Prevention of Cruelty to Animals (ASPCA), founded in 1866.

First cat show was held at the Crystal Palace in London in 1871. Since every cat thinks it's the most beautiful, they have shows in which humans make that choice.

First Westminster Kennel Club Show, the Oscars of the dog world, was held in 1877 in New York City.

First major horse show was also held in New York City, in 1883. It's sort of like a beauty pageant with hay.

First ostrich farm in the United States was built in Pasadena, California, by Edwin Cawston in 1886.

First animal movie star was the German shepherd Rin Tin Tin. He made his first movie in 1923 and went on to become one of the biggest screen successes of the era.

First modern guide dogs for the blind were trained in Germany in 1916 to aid World War I veterans. In 1928, a dog named Buddy became America's first Seeing Eye dog.

Animal Parade

Dogs, cats, and horses are part of our everyday lives, but many animals are just too wild to live in the suburbs or cities. They are still fascinating to look at, however. Here are some firsts from American zoos and animal exhibitions:

▶▶ The first lion exhibited in America was shown in Boston, Massachusetts, in 1716.

▶▶ America's first elephant arrived in New York City from India (by ship . . . it was too far to walk) in 1796.

▶▶ The first camel in America arrived in Boston in 1721; in 1856, 34 Turkish camels became the mounts for the first U.S. Army Camel Corps.

▶▶ America's first zoo opened in 1874 as the Philadelphia Zoological Garden.

▶▶ A frog named The Pride of San Joaquin won the first Calaveras County Frog-Jumping Contest in California in 1928. The event was inspired by a short story by author Mark Twain.

▶▶ Su-Lin was the first giant panda to come to the United States; she arrived in San Francisco, California, in 1936.

▶▶ The first hamsters bred in captivity gave birth to their first litter in Syria in 1938. All of today's pet hamsters are descended from these!

▶▶ America's first aquarium with space for large marine mammals, such as orcas and dolphins, was Marineland, which opened in 1938 in St. Augustine, Florida.

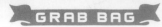

Amusement Parks

If you can't have fun at one of these places, then you just can't have fun! Amusement parks are located all around the world, supplying entertainment, thrills, and sore feet to millions! Here are the dates that some of America's biggest and most famous amusement parks first opened:

PARK, STATE	YEAR OPENED
Knott's Berry Farm, California	1920
Disneyland, California	1955
Busch Gardens (Tampa), Florida	1959
Six Flags Over Texas, Texas	1961
Universal Studios Hollywood, California	1964
Magic Mountain, California	1971
Walt Disney World, Florida	1971
EPCOT Center, Florida	1982
Legoland, California	1999

Nice Wheel, Ferris!

The Ferris wheel took its name from its inventor, George Washington Ferris. An engineer from Pittsburgh,

Pennsylvania, Ferris built a 250-foot (76-m) wheel in Chicago in 1893 for the World's Columbian Exposition. Some people thought that as soon as it started spinning, it would hop off its axle and roll through the city! Ferris and his wife climbed into the first car, which could hold more than 60 people, to take the first ride, proving that it was safe. The wheel was one of the hits of the exposition.

The First Roller Coaster

A former teacher named Lemarcus Adna Thompson created the first roller coaster in 1884. At a park in Coney Island, New York, he built a 450-foot (137-m) steel and wood track. The cars rocketed along at a hair-raising six miles (9.6 km) per hour! Okay, that's not that fast compared to today's speed-burners. But these wild rides had to start somewhere. Other inventors used Thompson's 1885 patent to make faster and bigger coasters. The first to top 60 miles (96 km) per hour was the all-wood Cyclone on Coney Island, which is still in operation.

MY FIRST...

The first amusement park I went to was _____

_____.

The first roller coaster I rode was _____

_____.

Here's what I thought about it: _____

_____.

Celebration Time!

Well, you all know when your first birthday was (if not, ask your parents!). But other holidays had different beginnings. Valentine's Day, for instance, began as a Roman festival honoring Juno, queen of the gods, and was renamed for St. Valentine in 496. The first April Fools' Day was celebrated in France in 1564. Here are the first years that some popular American holidays were celebrated:

HOLIDAY	FIRST CELEBRATION
Independence Day	July 4, 1781
Columbus Day	October 12, 1792
Memorial Day	May 3, 1868
Labor Day	September 5, 1882*
Arbor Day	April 10, 1872
Flag Day	June 14, 1877
Mother's Day	May 10, 1908**
Father's Day	June 19, 1910
Veterans Day	November 11, 1921
Earth Day	April 22, 1970
Martin Luther King Day	January 20, 1986

*Became national holiday in 1894   **Became national holiday in 1914

THE FIRST...

First Night

1

This alternative New Year's Eve celebration began in Boston, Massachusetts, in 1976, to wrap up the yearlong American Bicentennial. First Night events focus on community, the arts, performances, and magic acts. Since that first celebration, First Night has spread to more than 130 cities in four countries in 2005. (For more on New Year's events, see page 90.)

The First Thanksgiving

You've probably all heard the story of the first Thanksgiving feast, which happened in the British colony at Plymouth, Massachusetts, in the fall of 1621. The Plymouth Pilgrims were joined by Native Americans in a three-day feast honoring a good harvest. Congress began declaring national days of thanks in 1777 and for most years afterward, until President James Madison named two Thanksgivings in 1815. That slowed things down, thanks-wise, as there was not another official national Thanksgiving Day until 1863. A long campaign begun in the 1840s by Sarah Josepha Hale, a magazine editor, led President Abraham Lincoln to name November 26, 1863, as the first official national Thanksgiving Day. In 1939, the holiday was moved to its current spot on the calendar, the last Thursday in November. Turkeys everywhere wept.

On the Newsstand

For hundreds of years—before television, if you can believe there was such a time—most people got their world news through newspapers. Magazines were another important source of news and entertainment. They still are, of course, but now they compete with TV, radio, and the Internet. Here are some key firsts from the world of news:

Benjamin Harris published the **first newspaper in the American colonies**. The first (and only!) issue of his *Publick Occurrences Foreign and Domestic* was published on September 25, 1690. The **first American paper to be published regularly** was the *Boston News-Letter*, which debuted on April 24, 1704.

Pulitzer Prizes

When I first moved to New York City to be a writer, my friend Gordo sent me a card. On the front was a picture of a chicken, and inside it read, "We hope you win a Pullet Surprise!" ("Pullet" is a nickname for a type of chicken.) Why was that funny? Because there is a famous award given to writers, journalists, and playwrights called the Pulitzer Prize. Get it? Here are the winners of the first Pulitzer Prizes given in 1917 (the pullet and I are still waiting for our prize):

Reporting: Herbert B. Swope, *The World*

Editorial Writing: *New York Tribune*

History: J. J. Jusserand

Biography: Laura E. Richards and Maude Howe Elliott

First Issues of Popular Kids' and Teen Magazines

TITLE	YEAR	TITLE	YEAR
Boys' Life	1911	Sports Illustrated for Kids	1989
Highlights for Children	1946	Disney Adventures	1990
Sesame Street Magazine	1971	Nickelodeon Magazine	1993
Cricket	1973	Teen People	1998

The **world's first daily newspaper** was the *The Daily Courant,* which was first published in 1702 in England. The first daily paper in America was the *Pennsylvania Evening Post and Public Advertiser* of Philadelphia, which became a daily in 1783.

America's first newspaper sportswriter was Henry William Herbert, who covered outdoor sports (under the name Frank Forester) for several newspapers beginning in 1834.

Many people bought their daily newspapers in big cities from newsboys who carried bundles of papers around the city streets. The **first newsboy** employed by a big-city paper was Barney Flaherty, a ten-year-old who started selling for the *New York Sun* in 1883.

★EXTRA★

The **first photojournalist** (a reporter who uses a camera as well as, or instead of, writing) was Jacob Riis of the *New York Tribune* and the *New York Evening Sun*. In the late 1800s, his photographs were among the first published in newspapers and helped inspire improvements in living conditions for immigrants in the city.

Museums

Like the Scholastic Book of Firsts, *museums are chock-full of amazing stuff from all areas and all parts of the world. Some museums specialize in one thing or another, such as art or natural history. But all of them inspire, educate, amaze, and inform us. Here are some firsts from these wonderful places:*

❋The first public museum built to house a nation's treasures was the British Museum, which opened in 1753. It remains among the world's most amazing collections of valuable and rare objects from around the world.

❋America's first museum opened in 1773 in Charleston, South Carolina, originally focusing on items relating to South Carolina and its citizens.

❋Though there were small art galleries and public displays of art, the first major art museum in the United States was the Pennsylvania Academy of the Fine Arts in Philadelphia. Opening in 1805, it presented paintings and sculpture by European masters.

❋The world's first children's museum was the Brooklyn Children's Museum in New York City. It opened in 1899 with exhibits and displays aimed at young visitors.

❋Modern art includes works made beginning in the late 1800s that represent new styles of painting, drawing, and sculpture. In 1921, the Phillips Collection in Washington, D.C., became the first museum devoted to modern art alone.

❋The Portland Alien Museum in Oregon, which opened in 2003, was the first museum dedicated to the study of alien life and encounters with alien life. Do you have anything to send them (and we don't mean your sibling!)?

The Art World

Here you'll find groundbreaking moments in painting, sculpture, and mixed media . . . what are often called the fine arts. Below are a handful of arty firsts.

Among the many people to come to America with the early colonists was the **first artist in America**, Frenchman Jacques de Morgues Le Moyne. He landed in Florida in 1565. His 1565 painting of a meeting between a French settler and a Native American is considered the **first painting set in what would become the United States**.

The **first major American exhibit of modern art** (see page 166) was on February 17, 1913, in New York City. It was the first time many people in the United States had seen works by the major modern painters and sculptors.

The **first U.S. visit by the Mona Lisa** (right), the famous painting by Leonardo da Vinci, came in 1963; the painting was exhibited in Washington, D.C., and New York City, where it was viewed by millions of art lovers.

Some art can become very valuable to collectors. The **first sculpture to be sold for more than $10 million** at auction was *Petite Danseuse de Quatorze Ans* by Edgar Degas, which sold for $10.8 million in 1996.

The **first painting to top $100 million** at auction was *Boy with a Pipe*, by Pablo Picasso, which went for $104 million in 2004.

Theater

"All the world's a stage," wrote the famous English playwright William Shakespeare, "and all the men and women merely players." What he meant was that life can be seen as an ongoing human drama (or comedy, depending on your point of view). Here are some firsts from the world's stages:

534 BCE Thespis won the first Greek drama competition. That's why another name for actors is "thespians."

c. 800 The first drama school was established in China.

1520 The first permanent theater in Europe since Roman times was built in Malaga, Spain.

1589 William Shakespeare, the greatest playwright ever in the English language, produced his first play, called *Henry VI, Part I*.

1665 The first theatrical performance in the American colonies was given in Accomack, Virginia. Three men put on a short play in

 SAY IT FIRST...

first act Most stage plays or performances are produced from a script, written by a playwright, who includes all the dialogue (spoken words) and stage directions (telling actors where to move). Plays are usually divided into sections called "acts." The first act, then, is the first part of the play, in which the playwright usually sets the scene, introduces key characters, and begins the actions of the plot.

The First Tony Awards

Each year, the American Theater Wing and the League of American Theaters and Producers gives Tony Awards to the best plays, musicals, and performers on Broadway (the group of theaters around the New York City avenue of that name). The award is named for Antoinette Perry, an actress who had been president of the ATW. The Tonys were first awarded in 1947. Here are the first winners in key categories:

Actors (Dramatic): José Ferrer and Fredric March

Actresses (Dramatic): Helen Hayes and Ingrid Bergman

Author: Arthur Miller for *All My Sons*

Director: Elia Kazan for *All My Sons*

a park and were actually called a public nuisance and arrested for their efforts by an offended citizen. The charges were later dropped.

1690 *Gustavus Vasa*, by Benjamin Colman, was the first play written by a native of what would become the United States.

1750 *Richard III* became the first play by Shakespeare to be performed in America, in New York City.

1790 John Martin became the first native-born American to appear as a professional actor.

1866 *The Black Crook* was performed in New York City. It is regarded as the first true Broadway musical, a type of show that combines story, dialogue, music, and dance.

1905 Isadora Duncan opened the first modern dance school in the U.S. in New York City.

Dinosaurs

No one was around to take a picture of the first dinosaur, of course, but in the world of dinosaur fossils (paleontology), we can find some fascinating firsts. Scientists think there might be hundreds of other species of dinosaurs that have not been discovered yet. So keep looking—you might make your own "first" dinosaur find!

No one is quite sure what the **first dinosaur** was, but one candidate is the *Eoraptor*. Bones of this small, carnivorous dinosaur are the oldest ones yet found. They were dug up in Argentina and Brazil and are about 230 million years old.

In 1787, Caspar Wistar found a large thighbone near his home in New Jersey. He didn't know it at the time (and the fossil was later lost), but it was the **first dinosaur bone ever found in the United States**.

Also living in the time of the dinosaurs were huge reptiles that spent most of their lives in the water. Around 1810, Mary Anning of England was one of the **first people to find a fossil of an Ichthyosaurus**, one of those ancient reptiles. Anning became one of the most famous fossil hunters in the world.

In 1822, bones of another dinosaur were found in England. However, they were not named or recognized until 1825, when Gideon Mantell looked at the bones and some other teeth found with them and thought they looked like an iguana. He coined the term *Iguanodon*, making this the **first dinosaur to be discovered**, though another was called a dinosaur first (see page 171).

In 1824, William Buckland of Oxford University found the fossilized jawbone of a giant creature in England. He was the **first to identify the animal as an ancient reptile**. He named this first discovery *Megalosaurus*.

In 1842, Sir Richard Owen finally came up with a name for all of these reptile bones. He was the **first person to call these animals dinosaurs**. He combined the Latin words *deinos* (terrifying) and *sauros* (lizard).

In 1854, Benjamin Waterhouse Hawkins built the **first life-size model of a dinosaur**, out of concrete. He made an *Iguanodon* based on the skeletons found by Mantell and others.

In 1858, William Foulke unearthed the **first nearly complete dinosaur skeleton** in a mud pit in Haddonfield, New Jersey. Nearly all the bones except the skull were found; it was thought to be a *Hadrosaurus*.

The first *Tyrannosaurus rex* fossils were discovered by Barnum Brown in Montana, in 1902. Brown became one of the greatest dinosaur fossil hunters of all time. **T. rex was first named in 1905 by Henry Osborn**.

No one is completely sure what dinosaurs looked like on the outside, but an important discovery in 2000 gives some clues. Farmers in China discovered the **first dinosaur fossil covered with feathers**! Called a *dromeosaur*, this skeleton helps paleontologists continue their research on how dinosaurs and birds are related.

Buildings

Buildings are all around us—you're probably in one now, unless you enjoy reading outside. From tiny huts to huge convention centers, our cities and towns are filled with buildings of all shapes and sizes. The first buildings were probably made of wood, just sticks and logs stacked together to make a shelter. Early civilizations then developed bricks made of mud that were dried in the sun. Today, buildings are still made of those materials along with steel, iron, concrete, and glass. Here are some firsts among American buildings:

First brick building in America: It was built in 1633 as a home for the Dutch governor of New York, Wouter Van Twiller.

First marble building in America: Marble is a beautiful, hard stone used on many public buildings. The first such building in America was the Bank of the United States, which opened in Philadelphia in 1797.

Going Up?

As buildings began to get really tall, people needed a way—other than lots and lots of stairs!—to get themselves and their gear up all of those stories. So people looked at mechanical ways to go up and down. The first elevator was made by Henry Waterman in 1850. He used it to haul barrels into his shop in New York City. The key elevator first, however, came in 1853, when Elisha Otis (you'll still see his name in elevators you ride in) invented the safety brake—the first device that kept elevators from falling in case the ropes that pulled them up and down broke. In 1857, Otis installed the first enclosed elevator car in a store in New York. The patent for the first escalator, another way to move folks up and down, was granted to Nathan Ames in 1859.

First buildings with steam heat: It gets cold in Boston in the winter, and as engineers learned to use the new steam energy, they devised a way to send steam through pipes in a building. The hot pipes warmed up chilly rooms. The first building with steam heat was the Eastern Hotel in Boston, which opened in 1845.

First apartment house in America: Everyone in America lived in private homes until 1869, when the Stuyvesant Apartments opened on 18th Street in New York City. Each floor had four apartments.

First revolving door: This isn't a building, but it is a cool way to get into one! The first one was installed in a Philadelphia building in 1888.

First air-conditioned building: The Milam Building in San Antonio, Texas, which opened in 1928, was the first such building in the world. The first air-conditioned school, in San Angelo, Texas, didn't open until 1955, however, which doesn't seem quite fair!

First skyscraper: A skyscraper can be defined as a tall building with an internal skeleton of steel or iron. The first such building was the Home Insurance Building in Chicago, Illinois, which opened in 1885. It was built by William Le Baron Jenney and stood ten stories and 138 feet (42 m) tall. The first skyscraper in New York City, what is today home to the most skyscrapers in the world, was the 12-story Tower Building, which opened in 1889.

First building over 1,000 feet (300 m) tall: The Chrysler Building (right) in New York City, which opened in 1930, was the first building to reach above that lofty height.

First Across

The first bridge was probably a log that happened to fall across a stream somewhere. Some lucky caveperson found that they could cross the stream without getting wet and, ta-dah, bridges were born. At first, people used wood and stone to make bridges. Things have gotten a lot fancier since then, of course. Engineers use a wide variety of materials and an amazing assortment of designs to span waterways with huge bridges. Here are some fun firsts from the history of getting from here to there . . . without getting wet.

☛ The first writings about a bridge are from the Greek historian Herodotus, who described a wooden bridge supported by stone pillars over the Euphrates River in what is now Iraq.

☛ The first bridge in America, built in 1634, was over the Neponset River in Milton, Massachusetts.

☛ The world's first iron bridge went up in 1779. It was built over the River Severn in Coalbrookdale, England.

☛ The first iron wire suspension bridge was the Schuylkill River Bridge in Philadelphia. The 408-foot (124-m) span was built in 1816 at a cost of just $125! In this type of bridge, thick wires attached to towers hold up the road.

☛ The first steel suspension bridge was the famous Brooklyn Bridge (left) completed in 1883. Designers John and Washington Roebling (father and son) pioneered many bridge-building techniques to build it.

First Under

Gee, that's a big mountain in our way, we'd better go around it. That's what people thought most of the time . . . until they figured out how to dig through the mountain. And so tunnels were born to help people, ships, trains, cars, and more reach their destinations faster.

The **first tunnel in America** was built as part of a canal in Pennsylvania in 1821. The canal ran through the tunnel; the ceiling was high enough to let barges slide through.

The **first railroad tunnel in the United States** was built in Pennsylvania in 1834; it was more than 900 feet (274m) long.

The **first tunnel underneath a body of water in the United States** was a 1,520-foot (463m) tube that opened in 1869 beneath the Chicago River in Illinois.

The **first tunnel to go from the U.S. to another country** was between Detroit, Michigan, and Windsor, Ontario, Canada. At more than 5,000 feet (1,524m) long, it opened in 1930.

First Chunnel

For centuries, people in Great Britain and France dreamed of a tunnel that would go under the 17-mile (27-km) English Channel that separates their two nations. However, for most of that time, the two countries didn't like each other very much. Each feared that the other would use the tunnel to invade or to carry out military missions. Several attempts were made in the 1800s and early 1900s to move the idea forward, but they didn't get far. Finally, in 1987, the two countries agreed. In 1994, trains filled with passengers and cars zipped through the Channel Tunnel, or Chunnel, for the first time.

City Firsts

Believe it or not, there are many cities in the United States that use the nickname "City of Firsts" (though we don't know which was the first City of Firsts!). But that's not all; Eltham (also called Taranaki), New Zealand, is called the "Town of Many Firsts" (most of which involve cheese). We even found a Ciudad de Priméros in the Dominican Republic. Turns out, however, that many cities can boast firsts of their own, even if they don't use City of Firsts (those cities with a *) as one of their nicknames:

Baltimore*, Maryland: First American pro sports organization, the Maryland Jockey Club, formed in 1743; also home to the first YMCA, 1859

Boston, Massachusetts: First public park, Boston Common, 1634

Cincinnati, Ohio: First city university, 1870

Danville*, Kentucky: Birthplace of bluegrass music

Johannesburg, South Africa: The first discovery of gold here in 1886 helped create a gold rush that changed a small town into a major city.

Kokomo*, Indiana: Home of the first and only City of Firsts Visitors Center

Los Angeles, California: Home of the Kings, the first NHL team in California; they first played in 1967.

New York, New York: The first chess tournament held in the United States was the American Chess Congress, held here in 1857 and won by Paul Morphy.

Philadelphia, Pennsylvania: First World's Fair to be held in America, 1876, celebrating the 100th anniversary of the Declaration of Independence

Pittsburgh, Pennsylvania: First banana split made, 1904, which they could enjoy on the first Saturday holiday, which had begun in 1881, by the Westinghouse Company. Up to that point, everyone worked six full days a week!

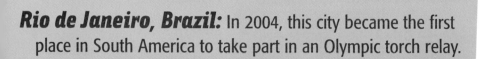

Rio de Janeiro, Brazil: In 2004, this city became the first place in South America to take part in an Olympic torch relay.

Santo Domingo*, Dominican Republic: First Caribbean nation with a hospital, university, fort, and cathedral

Shanghai*, China: This was the first city in China to have running water, telephones, automobiles, and movies.

Toronto, Canada: Norman Breakey of Toronto invented the paint roller in 1940.

SAY IT FIRST...

first America is certainly not the only place you can find firsts and English is not the only language to describe them. There is a whole world of firsts out there (some of them are in our book, but of course, we couldn't fit them all!).
So when you're out in the world, finding firsts, here is a handy chart listing how you say the word "first" in other languages:

Chinese (Mandarin)	diyi
Danish	først
Dutch	eerst
French	premier
Greek	proto
Hebrew	rishon
Icelandic	fyrstur
Italian	primo
Japanese	daishi
Latin	primo
Norwegian	for det første
Portuguese	primeiro
Spanish	primero
Swedish	första
Tagalog	pangunang lunas

CHAPTER 8

Groundbreakers

There are all kinds of people in the world, and this chapter looks at just some of those who were the first to break barriers, to bust down walls, and to break new ground for those who followed.

HIRAM REVELS

JANE ADDAMS

Female Firsts

Women have fought for centuries for equal treatment and respect. Here are some important American female groundbreakers in a wide variety of areas. You go, girls!

Margaret Brent: First woman in America to appeal for the right to vote, in 1647 in the colony of Maryland. Her request was denied.

Anne Bradstreet: First American woman writer; published a book of poems in 1650

Mary Kies: First American woman to be awarded a patent, 1809 (for a weaving technique)

Lydia Maria Child: First editor of first American children's magazine, *Juvenile Miscellany*, 1826

Arabella Mansfield: First woman to be admitted to practice law, 1869 in Iowa

Louise Bethune: First woman architect, 1881

Juliette Low: Founder and first president of the Girl Scouts of America, 1912

Jane Addams: First American woman to win the Nobel Peace Prize, 1931

Lettie Pate Whitehead (opposite page): First woman to serve on the board of directors for a major American corporation, The Coca-Cola Company, 1934

Pearl S. Buck: First American woman to win the Nobel Prize for literature, 1938

Ruth Hanna McCormick: First woman campaign manager for a presidential campaign, 1939–1940 (for Thomas Dewey)

Jerrie Mock: First woman to fly around the world solo, 1964

Elizabeth Hoisington and Anna Mae Hays: First female generals in the United States Army, 1970

Susan Roley and Joanne Pierce: First female FBI agents, 1972

Emily Warner: First female commercial airline pilot, 1973

Barbara Walters: First woman to be a network news anchor (main on-camera person), for ABC News, 1976

Mary Anne Dolan: First woman editor of major city daily newspaper, 1981 (*Los Angeles Herald-Examiner*)

Libby Riddles: First woman to win the 1,135-mile (1,827-km) Iditarod dogsled race in Alaska, 1985

Darlene Iskra: First woman to command a United States Navy ship, 1990

Janet Reno: First female U.S. attorney general, 1993

America³: First all-female crew to take part in an America's Cup qualifying race, 1995

Ms. Government

Men had been running the world for centuries—literally! Only in the past 150 years or so have women been allowed to take part in most government functions, whether in America or in other nations. Here are some barrier-breaking firsts from the history of women in politics:

592 Empress Suiko becomes the first woman to lead the empire of Japan.

1867 Lily Maxwell becomes the first woman to vote in a British parliamentary election.

Political Pioneers

U.S GOVERNMENT OFFICE	FIRST WOMAN, YEAR
Congressperson	Jeannette Rankin, Montana, 1917
Governor#	Nellie Tayloe Ross, Wyoming, 1925
Mayor (of large city)	Bertha Landes, Seattle, Wash., 1926
Senator*	Hattie Caraway, Arkansas, 1932
Cabinet member	Frances Perkins (Labor), 1933
U.S. ambassador	Eugenie Anderson, 1949
Supreme Court justice	Sandra Day O'Connor, 1981
Secretary of state	Madeleine Albright, 1996
President	We're still waiting. Do you want the job?

The first woman governor whose husband did not precede her in the office was Ella Grasso of Connecticut, elected in 1974.

* Elected to post, not appointed

1869 Wyoming becomes the first state to allow women to vote in local and state elections.

1872 Victoria Woodhull becomes the first woman to run for president of the United States when she is nominated for the office by the Equal Rights Party.

1893 New Zealand is the first country to grant all women the right to vote.

1907 Finland elects the first female members of Parliament.

1917 Russia's Aleksandra Kollontai is named Soviet commissar of social welfare, making her the first woman to hold a high-level national government office.

1920 For the first time, American women are allowed to vote in all elections, thanks to the ratification of the 19th Amendment to the Constitution.

1960 Sirimavo Bandaranaike of Sri Lanka is elected as the first female head of state.

1979 Margaret Thatcher is elected as the first female prime minister of Great Britain.

1985 Wilma Mankiller (right) of the Cherokee nation is elected as the first woman to be the chief of a major Native American tribe.

1993 Kim Campbell is elected as the first female prime minister of Canada.

IN THE FIRST PLACE...

Jackie Robinson

From 1884 until 1947, as major league baseball grew in popularity in the United States, African Americans were not allowed to participate in the majors. All that changed on April 15, 1947, when Jackie Robinson joined the Brooklyn Dodgers and broke baseball's "color" barrier as the first African American to play in the majors in the 20th century. Robinson's courage opened the door for the integration of all professional team sports in the United States.

Jack Roosevelt ("Jackie") Robinson was born in Cairo, Georgia, on January 31, 1919. A talented athlete throughout his youth in Pasadena, California, Jackie attended college at UCLA. There, he became the first student at that school to earn a varsity letter in four sports—baseball, basketball, football, and track.

After college, Jackie spent two years in the U.S. Army, then joined the Kansas City Monarchs of the Negro Baseball League, a league that gave black players the opportunity to play professional baseball. In 1945, Branch Rickey, president of the Brooklyn Dodgers, decided that he wanted to bring an African-American player into major league baseball. He chose Jackie Robinson, not only for his excellence as an athlete, but because he knew that Robinson had the strength of character to withstand the abuse that would be hurled at him as modern baseball's first black player.

In 1947, Jackie Robinson joined the Brooklyn Dodgers, becoming the first black player in the majors in more than 60 years (several black players had taken part in pro leagues in the 1880s). He put up with the jeers of some fans and the taunts of some fellow players.

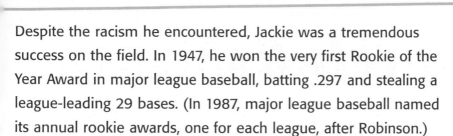

Despite the racism he encountered, Jackie was a tremendous success on the field. In 1947, he won the very first Rookie of the Year Award in major league baseball, batting .297 and stealing a league-leading 29 bases. (In 1987, major league baseball named its annual rookie awards, one for each league, after Robinson.)

Jackie Robinson went on to achieve many other firsts. In 1947, he became the first black player to play in a World Series. Two years later, he was the first black player to win the Most Valuable Player Award. Jackie Robinson retired in 1957 with a lifetime batting average of .311. In 1962, he became the first black player to be elected to the Baseball Hall of Fame. Jackie died in 1972.

In 1982, he became the first major league baseball player to be featured on an American postage stamp. Then, on April 15, 1997, the 50th anniversary of Robinson's groundbreaking achievement, the former Brooklyn Dodger became the first player to have his number (42) retired by every team.

Kid Firsts

Hey, kids can be groundbreakers, too! Here are some stories about the first kids to do some interesting things. Some of these kids got their firsts from luck or birth; others had to work hard to become the first in their fields. What have you been the first to do?

First kid born in the Americas: In about 1007, a group
of people from Iceland landed somewhere on the northeast coast of Canada or America. While they were there, a boy named Snorri was born, son of Thorfinn and Gudrid.

First kid born in what would become the United States: On August 18, 1587, Virginia Dare was born in the
British colony at Roanoke, in present-day North Carolina.

First kid author: In 1641, Francis Hawkins of England wrote
a book about manners called *Youth's Behaviour*. He knew what he was talking about because he was only eight!

First kid born in the White House: James Madison
Randolph was born on January 17, 1806. Why the White House? His grandpa was President Thomas Jefferson!

First kid to play in the majors: Joe Nuxhall was only
15 when he pitched in a baseball game for the Cincinnati Reds in 1944. Quite a jump from Little League!

First kid whose parents had both been in space:

Elena Andrionovna was born in 1964 to Soviet cosmonauts Valentina Tereshkova (see page 25) and Andrian Nikolayev.

First six-year-old college student: In 1990, Michael

Kearney started classes at Santa Rosa Junior College in California. That made him, according to the *Guinness Book of World Records*, the youngest college student ever.

First kid to pilot a plane across the Atlantic:

In 1994, Vicki Van Meter was 12 years old when she flew a Cessna 210 airplane from New York to England! (She wasn't by herself, but she was the main pilot.)

First kid to climb Mt. Everest:

In 2003, Ming Kipa, a member of the Tibetan Sherpa tribe, reached the top of the world's highest mountain when she was only 15.

First kid to win X Games gold: In 2003, Ryan

Sheckler, 13, took home the gold medal in the men's skateboard Park competition at the X Games in Los Angeles.

Author's Note: More than any nation in history, the United States is a mosaic of people from many lands and many backgrounds. The cool thing is that all these different people bring a wide range of experiences and cultures to our country.

On the next few pages, we'll celebrate some of our country's groundbreakers in a wide variety of fields.

African Americans

Congrats to these barrier-breaking African Americans from past and present:

First African American to . . .

. . . publish a book: Phillis Wheatley, *Poems on Various Subjects, Religious and Moral*, 1773

. . . found a major U.S. city: Chicago, Illinois, began in 1779 as a trading post established by Jean Baptiste Point du Sable, who was from Haiti, but whose parents had been from Africa.

. . . be a U.S. senator: Hiram Revels, elected in 1870 by citizens of Mississippi (see page 194)

. . . perform heart surgery: Daniel Hale Williams performed the world's first successful open-heart surgery in 1893 in Chicago.

. . . compete in the Olympics: George Poage, a runner in the 1904 Games

. . . become the world heavyweight boxing champion: Jack Johnson, who captured the title in 1908 and held it for almost seven years

. . . win a Pulitzer Prize: Gwendolyn Brooks won for poetry (*Annie Allen*) in 1950.

. . . win a major tennis tournament: Althea Gibson won at Wimbledon in 1957. Later that year, she became the first black player to win the U.S. Open.

. . . be named to the U.S. Supreme Court: Thurgood Marshall, 1967

. . . be the head coach of a major pro sports team: Player/coach Bill Russell, Boston Celtics, 1966

. . . be named chairman/CEO of a Fortune 500 company: Clifton Wharton (TIAA-CREF, a financial services company), 1987. (The Fortune 500 is a list of the world's largest companies in all business fields.)

. . . be elected as a state governor: Douglas Wilder, Virginia, 1990

. . . be named secretary of state: Colin Powell, 2001

Her Name in the News

In recent years, a number of African-American women have achieved notable firsts that earned them wide recognition in the media. Here's a partial list:

CATEGORY	FIRST AFRICAN-AMERICAN WOMAN, YEAR
U.S. senator	*Carol Moseley Braun* (Illinois), 1992
Astronaut	*Mae Jemison*, 1992
Winner of Nobel Prize for literature	*Toni Morrison*, 1993
National security adviser to the president	*Condoleezza Rice*, 2001
Academy Award for best actress	*Halle Berry*, 2001

Hispanic Americans

Let's salute these important primeros *by people who are united by language rather than by country of origin.*

First Hispanic American to . . .

. . . earn a medical degree in America: Jacob de la

Motta, 1789, from the College of Pennsylvania

. . . become a gold prospector in California:

Francisco Lopez discovered gold on March 9, 1842, in Los Angeles, more than six years before the more famous find in northern California started the Gold Rush.

. . . win the Congressional Medal of Honor:

Chilean-born Philip Bazaar, 1865, for actions during the Civil War

Señors Dinosaur

In 1979, father and son Luis and Walter Alvarez, both professors at the University of California at Berkeley, made an important discovery while studying rocks from a dig in Italy. Walter was a geologist, studying the composition of Earth, while Luis was a Nobel Prize–winning physicist. They discovered that the element iridium was present in large quantities during one particular time period. They felt that the iridium was not from around here (Earth, that is)—but, in fact, from outer space. Their discovery led them to become the first scientists to suggest that the extinction of the dinosaurs was primarily caused by a massive meteor strike on Earth. Not everyone agrees with this theory, but many point to it as an explanation for a great mystery.

. . . become a state governor: Romualdo Pacheco, California, 1875

. . . be elected to the U.S. Senate: Octaviano Larrazolo, New Mexico, 1928

. . . win an Academy Award for acting: José Ferrer, for *Cyrano de Bergerac*, 1950; Rita Moreno, for *West Side Story*, 1961

. . . be selected by NASA as an astronaut: Franklin Chang-Diaz, who made the first of his record seven shuttle flights in 1986; Ellen Ochoa, who first flew into space in 1993

. . . be named a cabinet secretary: Lauro Cavazos, secretary of education, 1988

. . . be inducted into the Rock and Roll Hall of Fame: Carlos Santana (right), 1998

. . . own a major league baseball team: Arte Moreno, an Arizona billionaire, purchased the Anaheim Angels in 2003.

Asian Americans

People have been coming from Asia to America for just over 150 years. Compared to some other groups, that's not that long, but this list of firsts is pretty impressive!

First Japanese person to enter the United States: Manjiro Nakahama, 1841. Only 15 years old, Manjiro was a shipwrecked sailor who landed in Hawaii and then traveled to Massachusetts to attend school.

First Asian-American citizen: Hikozo Hamada, originally from Japan, became a naturalized American citizen in 1850.

First Asian American to serve in Congress: Dalip Singh Saund, born in India, was elected to Congress from California in 1957.

A Real Groundbreaker!

The ancient Japanese sport of sumo wrestling dates back many centuries. For most of that time, only Japanese citizens could take part. A few wrestlers from other nations started to compete in sumo in the 1970s, however. In 1987, Hawaiian-born Salevaa Atisanoe became the first non-Japanese to reach the second-highest ranking in the sport, called ozeki or champion. Known as Konishiki, he weighed more than 640 pounds (290 kg) at his fighting peak!

First Asian-American senator: Hawaii's Hiram Fong took office in 1958 as one of the new state's first senators.

First Asian American to lead a major American orchestra: Seiji Ozawa took over the Boston Symphony in 1973.

First Asian-American governor: George Ariyoshi was elected governor of Hawaii in 1974.

First Asian-American general: United States Army Gen. John Liu Fugh attained that rank in 1984.

First Asian American to win an Academy Award: Haing Ngor, originally from Cambodia, won Best Supporting Actor for his work in *The Killing Fields* in 1984.

First Asian American in space: Astronaut Ellison Onizuka (above), a Japanese American, blasted off for the first time in 1985.

First Asian-American university president: Chang-Lin Tien, a Chinese American, was named the chancellor of the University of California at Berkeley in 1990.

Native Americans

Native Americans were the first people to live in North America and were the first to do many things on this continent. This page highlights just a few of the many modern firsts in Native American history:

First Native American West Point graduate:
David Moniac, a member of the Creek nation, graduated from the U.S. Military Academy in 1822.

First Native American senator:
In 1870, Hiram Revels, whose parents were African-American and Lumbee, a Native American tribe, was elected to the U.S. Senate from Mississippi (see page 188).

First Native American female physician:
In 1889, Susan La Flesche of the Omaha nation earned a medical degree from a college in Pennsylvania.

First novel by a Native American:
John Rollin Ridge, a Cherokee, published *The Life and Adventures of Joaquin Murieta. . .* in 1854.

First Native American international ballerina:
Osage ballerina Marjorie Tallchief was the first person from America to become the top dancer with the famous Paris Opera Ballet in 1957. She was also the first American to dance with Moscow's Bolshoi Ballet.

First Native American Medal of Freedom winner:
In 1963, Annie Dodge Wauneka, a Navajo tribal leader, was awarded the nation's highest civilian award for her contributions to tribal health care.

First Native American Pulitzer Prize winner:
N. Scott Momaday, a Kiowa/Cherokee, won the 1969 Pulitzer Prize for fiction for *House Made of Dawn*.

CHAPTER 9

Medicine

Open your book and say "aaah!" Time to take a trip to the doctor's and dentist's offices and examine some firsts from the world of stethoscopes (invented in 1816) and dental drills (first used in the United States in 1790). We promise this won't hurt a bit!

Medical History

Trying to figure out how our bodies work has perplexed people as long as there have been people. Trying to figure out how to fix bodies when something goes wrong has been nearly as baffling. Doctors and scientists have discovered many things about how the body works and have also created techniques and medicines to try and fix our bodies when illness strikes or an accident occurs. But it wasn't always this way. Read on for a look at some key firsts in the development of medicine:

First Hospitals

In India in about 500 BCE, the first clean, separate buildings for housing and treating sick people were built. The first hospital in the New World (the Americas) was built in Mexico City in 1524. America's first permanent hospital opened in Philadelphia in 1751 at the urging of Ben Franklin. (Several smaller clinics had been open as early as the 1660s in other cities.) Franklin was, as always, ahead of his time in recognizing the need for such a place in the growing American colonies. In 1854, the Nursery and Child's Hospital in New York City became the first children's hospital in the United States. The next year, the world's first hospital for women opened, also in New York.

First Vaccinations ("shots")

You can thank (or not) British doctor Edward Jenner the next time you get a shot at the doctor's. In 1796, he created the first vaccine (medicine made from germs and injected with a needle) for smallpox. It was the first ever and led to all of today's injected medicines. In 1952, American doctor Jonas Salk created the first vaccine against polio. In 1962, a vaccine against measles was introduced for the first time. The first vaccine against chicken pox was approved for use in 1995.

First Anesthetics

That's a tough word (it's pronounced "a-nes-THET-tics"), but it's a very important one. Anesthetics are medicines that knock out a person so that medical procedures can be performed without pain or discomfort. Imagine having an operation without them! That's how doctors worked for centuries. In 1842, Crawford Long, a doctor in Georgia, was the first to use ether during an operation. This chemical puts people into a deep sleep. Since then, other types of anesthetics have been developed.

First X-rays

One important medical tool was discovered by accident. Wilhelm Roentgen was conducting experiments with electricity in his lab on November 8, 1895. In the dark, he was shooting electricity through a glass tube. He was expecting a target in front of the tube to be lit up. Instead, a target lying on a table across the room lit up. He realized he had seen something no one else had seen—X-rays. His work led to the role of X-rays today, letting doctors look inside the human body. The first X-ray of a person was taken of Roentgen's wife's hand a month later.

A History-Making First

Scientists James Watson and Francis Crick made a discovery on March 7, 1953, that literally changed human history. They were the first to describe the structure of DNA, a chemical, which is found in the cells of our body, that carries our genetic information. Understanding what DNA is has helped scientists discover thousands of things about the human body and all living things. Impress your friends! Tell them DNA stands for deoxyribonucleic acid. Impress them more by saying it three times fast!

Office Visit

Doctors use many different tools in their work. Some of those tools are more familiar to you than others. But they haven't always been around. Here are the stories of how some of these instruments were first created:

First Microscope

Doctors can take a close-up look at all the little wriggly things in your blood and other places using a microscope. The first successful microscopes were built in the 1660s by Antony van Leeuwenhoek of Holland. He was the first to look at red blood cells and also to describe some of the bacteria that live in a person's mouth. While this was important to medicine, this was also the first time that people could see anything so small that it could not be seen with the naked eye. (Something that small is called microscopic.) Microscopes opened up a whole new world for people to discover. It was a world they had been living in the whole time, but had never been able to see.

First Thermometer

The famous Italian scientist Galileo Galilei constructed the first device that used liquid to measure temperature. His "thermoscope" showed general changes in temperature. In 1611, another Italian, Santorio Santorio, created a scale to use with Galileo's invention. This was the first thermometer, measuring temperature according to degrees on Santorio's scale. In 1724, Gabriel Fahrenheit of Germany invented the measurement scale for temperature named for him. In 1742, Anders Celsius invented the centigrade scale (commonly known as Celsius after ol' Anders).

First Stethoscope

Like many things in medicine, this familiar device has come a long way. The first stethoscope, created by a French doctor named René Laënnec in 1816, was just a hollow wooden tube. In 1852, American physician George Cammann made the two-eared version more familiar today.

First Blood Pressure Cuff

You know that pump thing they put on your arm at the doctor's? Made of rubber tubing, Velcro, and nylon, it fills with air and squeezes your arm while a doctor or nurse listens with a stethoscope. It is used to measure your blood pressure. Its official name is (take a deep breath) sphygmomanometer. Italy's Scipio Riva-Rocci made the first modern version of the spigmo—, um, sphygmet—, um, the device in 1896.

First Casts

Ever break a bone in your body? (We hope not!) Doctors use casts to hold some broken bones in place while they heal. The first casts were probably made of dried mud in ancient Egypt. In 1850, Dr. Anthonius Mathi of Holland developed a way to soak bandages in plaster. They hardened after being formed over the broken area. In 1972, lightweight fiberglass casts were first introduced.

Getting There Quickly

Wheeled carts were used for centuries to move wounded or sick people. But in 1796, Dominique Larrey of the French army made the first ambulance, a transportation device used solely for carrying people to get medical help. His wagon was drawn by horses, but was mounted on springs to make the ride safer and smoother for injured soldiers. Bellevue Hospital in New York City used the first horse-drawn ambulances in America in 1899. The French used the first motor ambulance in 1900.

Doctors and Nurses

Hard-working, dedicated, kind . . . plus they give out lollipops! They are the doctors and nurses of the world, using science and compassion to make us all feel better. Here are some famous firsts about medical professionals:

Doctor First?

All sorts of healers are found in every world culture. A 4,000-year-old handbook about medicine was found in a dig in Nippur (in present-day Iraq). But in the fourth century BCE, a Greek named Hippocrates was the first to treat sick people through a kind of early science. Instead of relying on spirits or "magic," as most early healers did, he tried to observe a patient and diagnose (decide what an illness is by the symptoms) what was wrong. He was also the first person to make the now-well-understood connection between our environment and our health. New doctors today recite the Hippocratic Oath, named for him.

First doctor in America: In 1610, the British colonists living in what would become Virginia welcomed Lawrence Bohune, a physician.

First African-American doctor in America: Dr. James Derham treated patients in New Orleans in 1790. In 1854, Dr. John de Grasse was the first African American to be admitted to a medical association,

when he was allowed to join the Massachusetts Medical Society. Rebecca Lee Crumpler became the first female African-American doctor when she received her degree in 1864.

First female doctor in America: In 1849, Elizabeth Blackwell graduated from a medical school in New York. Her sister Emily followed a year later.

First fully trained nurse in America: Nurses assisted doctors in many different ways at hospitals and offices. However, it was not until the late 1800s that a formal program to train nurses was created. Linda Richards was the first graduate of that program at the New England Hospital in 1872. In 1879, Mary Mahoney became the first African-American graduate of nursing school. (The first nursing school in the world was created in India in 250 BCE; only men were allowed to undergo training to care for the sick.)

MY FIRST...

My first doctor was named _____

_____.

My doctor checked my _____,

looked in my _____, and

counted my _____.

I was _____ years old the first time I got sick.

I lost my first tooth when I was _____ years old.

First Antibiotic

Antibiotics are important medicines that can kill germs that cause disease. Though other antibiotics were in use, it was not until 1928 that one was found to work against a wide variety of diseases. And it was found by accident! Scottish scientist Alexander Fleming saw a type of mold growing in a small dish. He found that this mold killed all sorts of harmful bacteria. He worked for more than a decade to get others to take his discovery seriously. In 1941, Ernst Chain and Howard Florey finally found that Fleming's mold, called penicillin, was a "miracle drug." With World War II raging, penicillin saved thousands of soldiers' lives. Since then it has saved millions and is perhaps the most important medicine yet discovered.

Stick to It

What is the one medical product that nearly every home has? And often with cartoon characters on it?! That's right—Band-Aids. That's the official trademark name of those little strips of tape and gauze that you put on cuts and scrapes. Thanks to Earle Dickson's wife, you can put a Band-Aid on your finger when you get a cut. Earle's wife was a bit accident-prone. Earle worked for Johnson & Johnson, a medical products company that, in those days, specialized in large gauze pads for surgery. In 1920, to help his wife with her many nicks and cuts, Earle cut up some of the large pads used in hospitals into smaller bits and stuck them to an adhesive strip of cloth. Company bosses knew a winner when they saw one and soon began producing Earle's strips by the millions. Johnson & Johnson estimates that more than 125 billion Band-Aids have been used worldwide since then.

E.R. Firsts

One good thing to come out of warfare was the idea of emergency medicine. Military doctors learned that immediate medical care greatly improved their patients' chances. The lessons learned with soldiers were put to work caring for civilians. Here are some firsts in emergency medical care:

1961 Four doctors at the Alexandria Hospital in Virginia became the first full-time emergency room (E.R.) doctors.

1967 Paramedics in Miami became the first to transmit EKG signals (which show how a person's heart is beating) from the field to a hospital.

1968 The first full-time trauma center (a kind of E.R. that offers very advanced care, often in large emergencies) opened in St. Vincent's Hospital in New York City.

1969 President Lyndon Johnson called for the first national paramedic testing standards, which were given in 1971.

1979 Emergency Medicine became an official specialty. Student doctors can now specialize in this important area.

SAY IT FIRST...

first responders Emergency personnel who are first on the scene of an accident. These are usually firefighters, but can also be police officers or paramedics.

First Blood

No one likes to see it, especially coming from yourself, but without blood, you just wouldn't get much done. Doctors have always known how important blood is. However, it took some creative people to invent blood banks, blood transfusions, and other lifesaving innovations.

1240 The Arab physician ibn al-Nasif was the first to note that blood moves from the heart to the lungs and back.

1628 William Harvey of England was the first to figure out that the heart pumps blood through the body.

1667 Doctors knew that if they could replace the blood a person lost following an injury or wound, the person might have a better chance of surviving. French doctor Jean-Baptiste Denis performed the first blood transfusion when he put a liter of blood from a lamb into a person. James Blundell got the bright idea of using human blood for the same purpose in 1818.

1921 In London, Dr. Percy Oliver came up with the idea for the first blood donation service, in which people could offer up a small amount of their own blood for use by others.

1931 In the Soviet Union, Dr. Sergei Yudin set up the first blood bank to supply Moscow hospitals. The first blood bank in the United States opened in Chicago in 1937.

1939 Charles Drew invented a system that can separate blood cells and plasma (the liquid part of blood). This means these blood products can be saved easily and for a longer time.

1979 In Japan, Dr. Ryochi Naito injected a person (himself!) with an artificial blood product for the first time. This substance can be used when no real blood is on hand.

Spare Parts

The human body is made of thousands of parts (some more important than others!). In the past 50 years, it has become possible for surgeons to replace some damaged body parts. This is done with transplants from human donors or with mechanical devices. Here are some firsts from this field:

💜 **First kidney transplant:** At Boston's Brigham Hospital in 1954, Dr. Joseph Murray successfully transferred a human kidney into a very ill person. An attempt in 1950 on identical twins had not been successful.

💜 **First hip replacement:** A broken hip used to mean life in a wheelchair for the patient. But in 1960, John Charnley of England put an artificial hip (made of steel and plastic) into a person for the first time. Because of these devices, patients suffering broken hips, who would have once been confined to a wheelchair, are now able to walk.

💜 **First lung transplant:** In 1963, James Hardy became the first doctor to do a lung transplant.

💜 **First heart transplant** (see page 206): The first heart transplant in the United States was performed in 1967.

💜 **First artificial heart:** In 1982, Robert Jarvik invented a plastic-and-metal pump that took the place of a person's heart.

Balloon Surgery

Your arteries carry blood from your heart to your body. In older people, these arteries can sometimes become blocked, leading to heart attacks. In 1964, Andreas Grüentzig, a German doctor working in Switzerland, performed the first operation to clear these blockages. In the procedure, called an angioplasty (AN-jee-oh-plass-tee), a small balloon is put into an artery. The balloon is carefully inflated to clear the blockage. And no, the balloon is not tied into the shape of a dachshund!

IN THE FIRST PLACE...

A New Heart

When someone dies, it is very sad. But thanks to some pioneering surgeons and brave patients, a person's death can also mean life for many others. Beginning in the 1950s, doctors began successfully transplanting small organs (see page 205). But transplanting a heart, the most important and complex organ, remained the ultimate goal.

The road to the world's first heart transplant was a long one, with several doctors taking some of the first steps. A key step was the invention of the first heart-lung machine in 1953. This machine keeps a patient's blood flowing and lungs breathing while surgeons stop the heart to operate on it. By 1967, the technology to do a heart transplant was beginning to be perfected. Several teams of surgeons felt they had the knowledge to do one. It was just a matter of finding the right donor heart and the right transplant patient.

On December 3, 1967, in Cape Town, South Africa, knowledge and timing came together. In an operation that changed medicine forever, Dr. Christiaan Barnard took a heart from the victim of a traffic accident and put it into the chest of an older man whose heart was failing. Hours later, for the first time in history, a doctor could say to his patient, "You've got a new heart."

Almost overnight, Dr. Barnard became an international celebrity. The world was fascinated with the operation. He flew

around the world appearing on TV and meeting with reporters and other doctors. Everyone wanted to know the details of this groundbreaking operation. And they wanted to meet the doctor who had made it happen.

What about the first heart transplant patient? Louis Washkansky would have died in a few days had he not undergone the operation. Yet his bravery would end up saving thousands of lives, even as he let himself become a sort of human experiment for the world. Washkansky lived for 18 days with his new heart before his diseased lungs failed. But those 18 days, and the operation that gave him those 18 days, changed the world. Since that first heart transplant, thousands of people have been given new life—with new hearts.

Dental Firsts

Time to go to the dentist! Wait . . . don't turn the page! We promise, this won't hurt a bit. Just lie back and open wide to take in this toothy pile of firsts from the world of tooth repair. Don't spit, please.

First fillings: The first person to suggest that cavities could be filled was an Arab physician named Rhezes. In about 900, he wrote that the diseased part of the tooth should be removed and a kind of cement put in the hole.

First rules for dentists: The first person to make dentistry a medical profession was Pierre Fauchard of France. Before then, people who fixed (that is, usually pulled!) teeth were barbers, doctors, or even blacksmiths. Fauchard created the first professional rules for dentists in 1696.

First false teeth: Though archaeologists have found false teeth in ancient ruins, the first ones that were professionally made and fit well were made of porcelain. Alexis Duchateau of France made them first in about 1770. In 1808, Italian Giuseppangelo Fonzi made

Goin' Drillin'

If you think dentists' drills are uncomfortable now, count yourself lucky you didn't live long ago. In about 200 BCE, Roman "dentist" Archigenes made the first dental drill by using a rope to spin a sharp stick. The first dental drill that was more than just a hand drill was invented in 1790 by John Greenwood of New York City. To operate it, a dentist stepped on a pedal that made the drill bit spin. In 1875, George Green invented an electric version. The first high-speed turbine drill (like the ones used today) was introduced in the United States in 1957. Patients breathed a sigh of relief.

the first versions that were held together with metal pins and kept in place by suction.

First American dentist: Josiah Flagg, the first dentist born in the United States, opened his practice in 1782 in Boston. At the time, he was 18 years old!

First metal fillings: In 1803, metal was used for the first time to fill cavities. Eventually, dentists settled on a mixture of different metals, such as silver, tin, and tungsten. Gold was also sometimes used; Philadelphia dentist Robert Arthur was the first dentist to use gold to fix teeth in 1855.

First dental school: In 1840, the first dental school in the world was the Baltimore College of Dental Surgery in Maryland.

First dental anesthesia: In 1844, Dr. Horace Wells used nitrous oxide ("laughing gas") on a patient for the first time. The patient? Himself! While Wells was under the influence of the gas, Dr. John Riggs took out one of his fellow dentist's teeth. Dr. John Morton is also credited with pioneering the use of anesthesia in dental work.

First female dentist: In 1866, Lucy Hobbs became the first woman to earn a degree in dentistry.

First book about orthodontics: In 1880, Norman Kingsley wrote a book about crooked teeth and how to fix them, creating a science called orthodontics. Thanks to his ideas (or no thanks, depending on your point of view!), dentists worked to perfect teeth-straightening devices that had been around in various forms for thousands of years.

First metal-wire braces: Thank astronauts for metal braces. During the 1960s, space technology developed a metal wire that was made more flexible by body heat. This meant it could be molded around teeth as part of braces.

Animal Doctors

Animals need medical care, too. The first descriptions of animal medicine can be found in ancient Egyptian scrolls. The Kahun Veterinary Papyrus, nearly 4,000 years old, describes all sorts of cattle diseases. The Code of Hammurabi from ancient Mesopotamia listed several rules for animal care, including how much these early vets could charge! Here are some firsts from the world of veterinary medicine:

First veterinary school: Founded by King Louis XV of France, it opened in France in 1762.

First American veterinary hospital: Charles Grice opened it in New York City in 1830.

First American with veterinary degree: In 1873, Daniel Salmon became the first American to earn a doctorate in veterinary medicine. He was a student at Cornell University. In 1910, Florence Kimball graduated from Cornell as the first woman with a veterinary degree.

First animal ambulance: The ASPCA operated the first ambulance for injured horses beginning in 1897 . . . two years before the first ambulances for humans!

First vet to win the Nobel Prize: Peter Doherty, trained as a veterinarian, won the 1996 prize for medicine for his work on how cells transmit diseases—in humans, that is. In 1976, another vet, Frederick Murphy, was the first person to see the deadly Ebola virus in a microscope. His work helped others contain and treat outbreaks of Ebola disease in humans and animals.

First animal blood bank: W. Jean Dodds opened Hemopet in southern California in 1985 to provide blood for injured animals and for animals facing surgery.

CHAPTER 10

Money

Cash . . . allowance . . . moola . . . bling-bling . . . whatever you call it, money makes the world go around. Okay, really gravity makes it go around, but you know what we mean. In this chapter, discover a fistful of money firsts.

Early Money Firsts

Money was not invented by one person or civilization. The idea of trading something of value for something you need grew up bit by bit in cultures all around the world. Eventually, people figured out that using coins or cash worth, say, 10 cows or 100 bushels of wheat was easier than carrying cows or wheat in your wallet or purse!
Here are some key firsts from the early development of money:

First Coins

King Croesus of Lydia, an ancient kingdom in what is present-day Turkey, created the first coins in about 678 BCE. They were small gold and silver disks stamped with the king's seal. This proved to everyone who used them that they had value. Greek historian Herodotus also wrote that the people of Lydia were the first to open permanent shops. They had to have a place to spend all those coins, right?

First Official Nonmetal Money

Looking for a handier way of carrying around their treasure, Chinese emperors issued pieces of white deerskin about a foot (26 cm) square. Each piece was worth 40,000 regular coins—to say nothing of being much easier to carry than 40,000 coins!

First Paper Money

Once again, the Chinese were innovators in money. During the reign of Emperor Hein Tsung in the early 800s, the country had a shortage of copper, the metal used in making the empire's coins. The emperor ordered the creation of the first paper money.

First National Currency

One problem with early money is that there were so many

different coins from so many different places that no one knew what was worth what. England is one example. There were several smaller kingdoms on the island. They each issued their own coins. In 928, led by a king named Athelstan, all the kingdoms signed the Statute of Greatley. For the first time, they agreed there should be one kind of money for the whole island.

First Milled Coins

When you have money around, unfortunately, you also have crooks. As soon as governments started making coins, thieves started making copies. But they needed metal. One way they got metal was by clipping off the edges of coins, melting the pieces down and then casting new coins. In 1645, the mint (a place where coins are made) in Paris, France, made the first coins with milled edges. An example of a milled coin is a U.S. quarter; the ridges on its edge are made by milling. With milling, thieves could not shave off metal without their work being noticed.

First Wooden Coins

When the bank in Tenino, Washington, closed in 1932, the town had no cash. Citizens agreed to use wooden coins in trade.

First Place to Use Gigantic Stone Disks for Money

Okay, this is a bit of a stretch because the Pacific island of Yap is probably the ONLY place where a type of money is made from giant rocks that look like humongous grocery cart wheels. But they were still first! Talk about having a tough time holding on to your money—some of the rock disks were as large as 12 feet (3.4 m) tall!

American Currency

One of the first things that the young United States did was make its own money. This is one of the key responsibilities of any government. In the case of the United States, it was a way for the new nation to set itself apart from Great Britain. What happened first in American money? Read on to find out. . . .

In 1637, Massachusetts colonists were the first European settlers to create a form of money for use in what would become America. The colonists declared the Native American form of money called wampum, made of seashells linked together, to be the **first colonial "legal tender."** That means paper or coinage that a society agrees has a certain worth. Check out a dollar bill; see if you can find those words on it, even today.

In the early days, some U.S. states and colonies issued their own money. In 1786, New Jersey put out the **first coins with the slogan "E Pluribus Unum."** This means "from out of many, one," and is still a part of all American coins.

In 1792, for the first time, the U.S. Congress chose the "dollar" as the **first official American currency**. A dollar was then divided into 100 cents. This was to make it clear that British money—which did not use a 100-cent decimal system—was no longer welcome in the good ol' U.S. of A.!

That same year, Congress built the **first U.S. Mint**. A mint is a place where coins and paper money are made. The first U.S. Mint was built in Philadelphia. It was also the first new U.S.

government building of any type. President George Washington appointed David Rittenhouse as the first director of the Mint. The *first coins made by the Mint* were 11,178 copper cents in March 1793. These one-cent coins were actually larger than today's quarters.

Current U.S. Coins

Here is the date of the first appearance of coins currently in use in the United States:

COIN	PERSON ON COIN	FIRST ISSUED
Penny	Abraham Lincoln	1909
Nickel	Thomas Jefferson	1938
Dime	Franklin Roosevelt	1946
Quarter	George Washington	1932
Fifty-cent piece	John F. Kennedy	1964
Dollar	Susan B. Anthony	1979*
Dollar	Sacagawea	2000**

* Susan B. Anthony was the first real woman to be featured on a U.S. coin. A female figure representing "Liberty" appeared on many coins, but was not based on a real person.

** The infant son of Lewis and Clark's guide, Sacagawea, shown on this gold-colored coin is the first child to appear on official U.S. money.

Over There

For many years, each European country made its own kind of money. But in 1999, the European Union, a group of nations, began using the same kind of money. On January 1, 1999, 11 nations started using the euro as their official currency. Those first 11 countries were Belgium, Germany, Spain, France, Ireland, Italy, Luxembourg, Austria, Finland, the Netherlands, and Portugal.

U.S. Paper Money

Coins are fun and jingly and perfect for buying bubble gum or playing video games at the arcade. But, as the folks back in China (see page 212) learned, all those coins can be heavy, too. Paper money is much more portable. Here are some firsts from the history of paper money in America:

First Official Paper Money

In 1690, the Massachusetts Bay Colony issued the first official paper money in the colonies. The first people to get this money were some colonists who had been sent on a military trek to Canada. When they came back, they were paid with the cash. All Massachusetts residents and merchants were required to accept the cash in exchange for goods.

First Paper Money in the Colonies

The Continental Congress organized the War for Independence, also known as the American Revolution. As they built their army, they had to find a way to pay the soldiers. In 1775, they created the first American paper money, $2 million worth of notes called "Continentals." That was good news for the soldiers. The bad

news was that the Continentals could not be turned in for silver or gold until after the war—which didn't end until 1781!

First United States Paper Money

Following the signing of the Declaration of Independence, the colonies had a new name, so it was time for new money. In 1792, for the first time, paper money was issued bearing the words "The United States." To make sure people knew the bills were genuine, famous figures from the American Revolution signed each bill.

First Person on a U.S. Bill

All those early versions of American cash had only designs or symbols on them. They did not have the familiar faces we see on our money today. The first person to get his picture on U.S. money was Treasury Secretary Salmon P. Chase. His face appeared on a dollar bill issued on March 10, 1862. The first president's face to appear on a bill was Abraham Lincoln, whose $10 bill came out later the same year.

First Year for Current Size Bills

Until 1929, U.S. paper money came in varying sizes, most larger than the size we use today. In 1929, for the first time, all paper money was made the same size. Also, for the first time, portraits of notable Americans appeared on all denominations (dollar values). On the bills' backs are buildings in Washington, D.C.

Really Rich People

So, who has all this money? Well, thanks to their own hard work—or that of their parents!—or sometimes to just luck, some folks have big, heaping piles of money. Here are some firsts from the wonderful world of wealth.

First American worth more than $100 million:
In 1877, shipping tycoon Cornelius Vanderbilt's estate topped that magic mark.

First American billionaire: In 1911, Standard Oil
founder John D. Rockefeller's fortune was estimated to be well over $1 billion.

First woman millionaire: Sarah Breedlove, known as
Madame C. J. Walker, created a line of cosmetics for African Americans in 1905. Women had been millionaires before, but their money came from inheritance or from their husbands. Walker was the first "self-made" female (and first female African-American) millionaire.

First African-American millionaire: A native of
the Virgin Islands named William Leidesdorff probably holds this title, but he never knew it. He was a California landowner and shipowner. When he died in 1848, his estate actually owed money. But about a year later, gold was found on some of his land, which instantly made his estate worth millions of dollars. Too bad he wasn't around to enjoy it!

First TV millionaires: The first person to win the
biggest prize on *Who Wants to Be a Millionaire?* was on the British version. In early 1999, Judith Keppel won one million British pounds, worth about $1.4 million. The first U.S. $1 million-winner was John Carpenter the same year.

Stamp Firsts

Believe it or not, until the middle of the 1800s, if you mailed something, the person who received it had to pay the postage. We're glad that's not true today—think of how much money junk mail would cost you! Anyway, a schoolteacher in England named Rowland Hill had the bright idea to charge for sending mail. Hill came up with a way to prove a person had paid—sell them a stamp. He invented that sticky little piece of paper in 1837. Here are some sweet stamp firsts:

First stamp: The British "penny black" in 1840

First U.S. Post Office stamps: In 1847, a 5-cent red stamp depicted Benjamin Franklin, while George Washington's portrait appeared on a 10-cent black stamp.

First perforated stamps: The 1-cent Franklin blue stamp of 1857 was the first with those handy little holes along the edges that make stamps easier to separate.

First U.S. stamp showing a woman: An American stamp issued in 1893 in honor of the 500th anniversary of Columbus landing in the Americas showed Spain's Queen Isabella.

First African American on a stamp: Abolitionist and educator Booker T. Washington in 1940

First living American on a stamp: Postal regulations say that a person must be dead at least ten years before he or she is eligible to appear on a stamp. An exception was made in 1969 to show astronaut Neil Armstrong's historic Moon landing.

U.S. Postal Firsts

The Continental Congress named Benjamin Franklin the first colonial postmaster general in 1775.

In 1789, Samuel Osgood became the first official United States postmaster general.

The first Pony Express ride left St. Joseph, Missouri, on April 3, 1860. Records from the time name seven men as the first riders, but most agree the first horse's name was Sylph. The relay race of riders carried mail to the western United States, before the telegraph (see page 266) knocked it out of business just over a year later.

The first mail delivered by dogsled arrived in Montreal, Canada, from Lewiston, Maine, in 1929.

The first official airmail pilot was Earl Ovington, who got the job in 1911.

ZIP codes were first used on July 1, 1963. The expanded "ZIP-plus-4" codes debuted in 1983.

SAY IT FIRST...

first-day cover Stamp collectors prize a postage stamp bought and used on the first day that it is available to the public. Such collectibles are called "first-day covers." These stamps receive special cancellations (the circular mark that shows a stamp has been used) on that day. Often, specially decorated envelopes are sold with additional art and information about the stamp's subject.

Collecting Firsts

Many people collect coins or stamps as hobbies. Coin collectors are called "numismatists" while stamp fans are known as "philatelists." There, now you can say you learned some new words today! You're welcome! Collectors hope that the coins and stamps they collect will become worth much more money over time. Here are some firsts from the big-money world of collecting coins and stamps:

The **first book on coin collecting,** *A Treatise on Coinage,* was written in 1149 by the Chinese writer Hong Cun.

The **first U.S. postage stamps to sell at auction for more than $1 million** earned that price thanks to a mistake. In 1918, a sheet of 24-cent airmail stamps was issued showing an airplane (a JN-4 biplane, or "Jenny," if you must know) in the center. One sheet was printed with the airplane upside-down and mistakenly sold to a wise stamp collector. In 1989, four of those stamps, known as the "Inverted Jenny," were sold together for $1 million.

The **first coin to sell for more than $1 million** was a 1913 nickel, which sold for $1.4 million in 1996. The first coin to sell for more than $7 million was a 1933 U.S. double eagle gold coin. It sold for $7.59 million in 2001.

The **first foreign stamp to sell for more than $2 million** came from Sweden. Originally worth only two skillings (an old form of Swedish money), it was printed on the wrong color paper, yellow instead of green. There is only one of these stamps still known to exist, and it sold for $2.3 million in 1996.

Pay with Plastic

The invention of plastic and the use of computers and other digital devices meant that people did not have to pay cash for everything they bought. Beginning in the 1950s, credit cards changed the way people spent money. Credit cards work like this: The user gives the card to a merchant, who records the card number and the total. The credit card company pays the merchant, while the user pays the credit card company . . . eventually. Anyway, here are some fun firsts from the history of plastic money:

In 1950, the Diners Club issued the **first nationally accepted credit card**. It was invented by Diners Club founder Frank McNamara. The card was accepted only in some restaurants in major cities in the United States. Some department stores had earlier issued credit cards, but these cards could only be used at their stores.

In 1958, the **first American Express card** was issued. In addition to an annual fee, users had to pay their entire credit card bill each month.

Later in 1958, Bank of America put out the **first bank credit card**. It was called the BankAmericard (it changed its name to Visa in 1976). Its big innovation was that people could pay less than the full amount they owed each month. The bank then charged them interest (a small percentage of the money owed) for the privilege of delaying payment.

The **first debit cards** were issued in the 1990s as single-store cards. Banks started using debit cards, too, in 1997.

Stock Stuff

Companies sell off parts of themselves by selling shares of stock. These shares are bought and sold by investors. Most hope that the value of their stocks will go up, thus earning them more money (and a place on page 218!). This selling and buying happens at a stock exchange. Get out your checkbook and read about some firsts in stock history:

The **first stock exchange in the world** opened in Antwerp, Belgium, in 1460.

The **first company formed by selling shares of itself** was the Russia Company, started in England in 1553. Investors used the money to pay for trading expeditions to Russia and Asia.

The New York Stock Exchange (NYSE), the **first stock exchange in the United States,** opened on May 17, 1792.

The Dow Jones Industrial Average (DJIA) measures the overall success of the NYSE. The average is made up of the cost of the shares of 30 large companies. The **first DJIA was released in 1896,** and its first average was 40.94. That average is now based on a really complicated equation. The higher the number is, the better. Here are some key DJIA firsts:

First time the DJIA rose above . . .

1,000	November 14, 1972
5,000	November 21, 1995
9,000	April 3, 1998
10,000	March 29, 1999

Bank on It

From piggy to First National, banks are where we keep our money. Here are some firsts from the world of banking:

Who created bank checks? Dutch traders of the 1400s probably created the first system of uniform checks; that is, written the same way by everyone. The earliest example of a check (or "cheque") written in England is an order to a goldsmith called Morris and Clayton to pay a Mr. Delboe 400 pounds ($750). The first printed checks were created in England in 1762 by Lawrence Childs.

What was America's first bank? In 1781, needing a way to finance the Revolutionary War, the Continental Congress opened the Bank of North America in Philadelphia.

What was the first international bank? In 1945, 21 countries chipped in money to create the International Bank for Reconstruction and Development.

Who sold the first traveler's checks? Marcellus Berry of the American Express Company thought up this bright idea in 1891. Instead of carrying cash, travelers could carry checks, which could be replaced if lost or stolen.

Where was the first bank drive-through? Does your town have one of these? They're pretty slick; the customer stays in his or her car while sending documents back and forth to the teller, sometimes through vacuum tubes. The first was built for the Exchange National Bank in Chicago, Illinois, in 1946.

What bank had the first ATM (automatic teller machine)? Today, of course, they're everywhere. But the first was at a Chemical Bank in Rockville Center, New York, in 1969.

CHAPTER 11

Sports

Kick it, throw it, catch it, hoop it, race it, ace it, or even put a gold medal on it . . . this chapter dives into the wonderful world of sports—and finds that there is more to sports than just finishing in first place!

Play Ball!

Take us out to the ball game! Baseball's roots can be traced to several English games that used sticks and balls (one of the most popular was called "rounders"). After baseball's rules were finally written down, it became the first professional team sport in America. Along with giving millions of kids hours and days of fun, baseball has been an important and popular part of American culture since before the Civil War. Here are some of the key firsts in the development of the "national pastime":

1st The first set of standard baseball rules was written in 1845 by the Knickerbocker Base Ball Club of New York. The club was created by Alexander Cartwright and Daniel Adams.

1st The first organized baseball game was played on June 19, 1846, at the Elysian Fields in Hoboken, New Jersey. The Knickerbockers were beaten at their own game! They lost to the New Yorks, 23–1, in four innings.

1st The first professional baseball team was the Cincinnati Red Stockings, who played their first game on March 15, 1869. They beat Antioch College, 41–7. The Red Stockings were the first team to pay all their players.

1st The first major league was the National League (N.L.), founded in 1876 with eight teams. The American League joined the N.L. as a major league in 1901.

1st In the first major-league game, between two N.L. teams, the Boston Red Stockings beat the Philadelphia Athletics, 6–5, on April 22, 1876. In that game, Jim O'Rourke of Boston got the first major-league hit.

The World Series

The first event called the World Series was played in 1884, but it was between an N.L. team and the champion of a minor league. The World Series as we know it today, between the champions of the A.L. and N.L., was first played in 1903. The first World Series champion was the Boston Americans (now known as the Red Sox, of course), who beat the Pittsburg (that's how they spelled it then) Pirates. Here are some other World Series firsts:

First home run: Jimmy Sebring, Pittsburg Pirates, 1903

First stolen base: Honus Wagner, Pittsburg Pirates, 1903

First pitcher to hit a Series homer: Jim Bagby, Sr., Cleveland Indians, 1920

First grand slam: Elmer Smith, Cleveland Indians, 1920

First World Series on the radio: 1922

First televised World Series: 1947

First no-hitter: Don Larsen*, New York Yankees, 1956

First World Series MVP: Johnny Podres, Brooklyn Dodgers, 1955

First manager to win in both leagues: Sparky Anderson, Cincinnati Reds (N.L., 1975) and Detroit Tigers (A.L., 1984)

First winning team from Canada: Toronto Blue Jays, 1992

First wild-card champion: Florida Marlins, 1997

*First and only perfect game in World Series history

Baseball Hardware

The best baseball players earn special awards (they call the trophies "hardware"). Here are some baseball award firsts:

Most Valuable Player

Originally called the Chalmers Award, it was first presented in 1911. Since 1931, an MVP for each league has been chosen by the Baseball Writers Association of America.

First N.L. Winner: Frank "Wildfire" Schulte, Chicago Cubs, 1911. **First A.L. Winner:** Ty Cobb, Detroit Tigers, 1911. **First Back-to-Back Winner:** Jimmie Foxx, Philadelphia A's, 1932–33. **First Winner, Three Straight Years:** Barry Bonds, San Francisco Giants, 2001–2003; also first player to win six awards

Cy Young Award

This award for the top pitcher in each league is named for Cy Young, who was the first pitcher to win 400 games and then 500 games, and the first to lose 300 games! Here are some Cy Young Award firsts:

First Winner: Don Newcombe, Brooklyn Dodgers, 1956 **First Six-Time Winner:** Roger Clemens (Boston Red Sox, Toronto Blue Jays, New York Yankees) **First Winner, Four Straight Years:** Greg Maddux, 1992–95 (Chicago Cubs, Atlanta Braves)

Rookie of the Year Award

The first nationally recognized rookie of the year award was given in 1947 to Jackie Robinson of the Brooklyn Dodgers. In 1987, baseball named this annual award (now given to one player in each league) after Robinson (see page 186).

The Bambino

George Herman "Babe" Ruth—known as "The Bambino" and "The Sultan of Swat"—is still probably the most famous baseball player of all time. He hit his first homer in 1915—as a pitcher! In 1919, he set his first home run record with 29 dingers. In his 21-year career, Ruth racked up—along with a reputation as one of the biggest eaters in baseball history!—many firsts:

Babe was . . .

. . . the first player with 30, 40, and 50 homers in a season: 1920

. . . the first player with 60 homers in a season: 1927

. . . the first player to homer in Yankee Stadium: April 18, 1923

. . . the first to reach 500, 600, and 700 career home runs

The All-Star Game

In 1933, playing in the first All-Star Game, Babe Ruth hit the first-ever home run in what would come to be called the "Midsummer Classic" between the best from the A.L. and N.L. Here are some other All-Star Game firsts:

First game: A.L. beat N.L., 4–2, on July 6, 1933, Comiskey Park, Chicago

First All-Star MVP: Maury Wills, L.A. Dodgers, 1962

First two-time MVP: Willie Mays, San Francisco Giants, 1963, 1968

First grand slam: Fred Lynn, California Angels, 1983

Around the Horn

The title of this page is a baseball term for a double play that goes from the third baseman to the second baseman to the first baseman. It covers all the bases! These pages "touch 'em all" (a phrase heard from some announcers when a player hits a homer) while covering a wide variety of baseball firsts.

First (and only!) World Series unassisted triple play: Bill Wambsganss, Cleveland Indians, 1920

First box score: The first detailed summary of statistics from a particular game was printed in box form in June 1853 in the *New York Clipper*. It was the creation of *Clipper* sportswriter Henry Chadwick.

First presidential pitch: The first president of the United States to throw out the first ball on Opening Day was William Howard Taft in Washington, D.C., on April 14, 1910.

First singing of the national anthem at a game: "The Star-Spangled Banner" was sung for the first time at a sporting event in the middle of the seventh inning of Game 1 of the 1918 World Series between the Boston Red Sox and the Chicago Cubs at Chicago's Comiskey Park.

First uniform numbers: The New York Yankees, in 1929. Starting players were given numbers that matched their usual place in the batting order. That's why Babe Ruth, who batted third, wore number 3, and Lou Gehrig,

the cleanup hitter, wore number 4. Pitchers were given numbers 10 and higher.

First designated hitter: In 1973, A.L. teams began using a D.H. to take the pitcher's regular turn at bat. The first D.H. was Ron Blomberg of the New York Yankees, playing on April 6, 1973. He drew a walk.

First player to play all nine positions in one game: Bert Campaneris, Kansas City Athletics, September 8, 1965. He played one inning at each position.

First player to "use his head" to help a homer: Jose Canseco hit many huge home runs. In 1993, he was on the other end of one—in a funny way. While playing outfield for Texas, Canseco misplayed a long fly; the ball bounced off his noggin and over the fence without hitting the ground! It was a homer for the batter and a headache for Jose.

Behind the Plate

Catchers wear more equipment than any other player on the field. Here are some firsts about their gear. (What is most amazing about these is how long it took them to figure out that wearing it would be a good idea! Ouch!):

☛ Fred Thayer of Harvard University patented the first catcher's mask in 1878.

☛ The wife of Detroit Tigers catcher Charles Bennett made the first catcher's chest protector around 1886 for her husband.

☛ New York Giants catcher Roger Bresnahan wore a set of leg pads typically worn by cricket players in a 1907 game, becoming the first catcher to wear shin guards.

In the Ballpark

Here are some firsts from the world of ballparks and stadiums:

First ballpark hot dogs: Two stories describe the first appearance of this classic ballpark food. One story says that the first hot dogs at ballparks were found in St. Louis in 1893; another version says that vendor Harry M. Stevens first served hot dogs at the Polo Grounds in New York in 1901.

First ballpark where fans could keep foul balls: This tradition started at what was then called Weeghman Park (later Wrigley Field) in Chicago in 1913.

First night game: The Cincinnati Reds were the first major league team to play under lights when they hosted the Philadelphia Phillies on May 24, 1935.

First indoor game: The Houston Astros open the Astrodome on April 9, 1965, with an exhibition game against the New York Yankees.

Women in Baseball

Kathryn Johnston of Corning, New York, was the first girl to play Little League in 1950, by posing as a boy. But in 1951, Little League changed its rules to keep girls out. In 1974, the rules were changed again, and the first girl to officially play in Little League was Maria Pepe in Hoboken, New Jersey. In 1989, Julie Croteau became the first woman to start for a men's college team, when she played first base for St. Mary's College. In 1994, outfielder Kendra Hanes was the first woman on a professional minor league team, the Kentucky Rifles in the Kentucky Frontier League.

Kids' Stuff

In 1939, Carl Stotz of Williamsport, Pennsylvania, rounded up 40 neighborhood kids to form the "The Williamsport Little League." Since then, Little League has grown to include leagues in more than 100 countries. It's not the only youth baseball program, but it is the largest and oldest. Each August, the Little League World Series is held to determine the best team of 11–12-year-olds. Here are some Little League firsts:

First Little League World Series:
1947, Maynard Midgets (Penn.) beat Lock Haven (Penn.), 16–7

First international champion: Monterrey, Mexico, 1957

First championship perfect game: Angel Macias, Monterrey, Mexico, 1957

First Little Leaguer to reach major leagues:
Joey Jay of Middletown, Conn., who played for the Milwaukee Braves in 1953

First Little Leaguer elected to the Baseball Hall of Fame: Jim "Catfish" Hunter, Oakland A's/New York Yankees, 1987

First player to play in both Little League and Major League World Series: Jim Barbieri (Schenectady, N.Y., 1954 and Los Angeles Dodgers, 1966)

First Little Leaguer to become president of the United States: George W. Bush, who played catcher for the Midland Cubs (Texas) in the 1950s

Hoop It Up!

Most sports are not invented; instead, they evolve from different games into the sports we know today. Not basketball, though. Hoops dribbled out of the imagination of one man in one day! In 1891, Dr. James Naismith, a P.E. teacher at Springfield College in Massachusetts, was looking for a way to keep his students busy indoors during the winter. He came up with 13 rules for the first basketball game. How cool is that? Have you ever invented a sport? Here are some firsts from basketball's early days:

First game: December 15, 1891, between 18 students in Naismith's class. William Chase scored the first (and only) basket of that game, worth one point.

First name: The sport was called Naismith Ball at first. Um, glad they changed the name, huh?

First public game: Played on a YMCA court with peach baskets set up at either end, on January 20, 1892. There were nine players to a side and a basket was worth one point.

First college game: Minnesota State School of Agriculture defeated Hamline College of St. Paul, Minnesota, 9–3, in 1895.

First game, five-man teams: The University of Chicago beat the University of Iowa, 15–12, on January 16, 1896. Until this game, teams had anywhere from six to ten players; this game

Ambassadors of Basketball

By the 1930s, basketball boasted more than 20 million fans worldwide. A big reason was the Harlem Globetrotters. The team that would become known as the "clown princes of basketball" played their *first game* on January 7, 1927, in Hinckley, Illinois, before a crowd of 300. They combined outstanding basketball talent with crowd-pleasing jokes, games, and skits. In 1985, Lynette Woodard, an All-America at Kansas, became the *first woman to play for the Globetrotters*. The team continues to thrill millions each year.

established five as the standard number. (Chicago coach Amos Alonzo Stagg had played in the first public game in 1892!)

First international champ: The first pro basketball players were organized as teams, not leagues. The teams traveled the country playing against other local teams and shared the money from tickets sold. One successful team was the Buffalo Germans, who began in 1895. They won the first international basketball tournament, held in St. Louis as a demonstration sport during the 1904 Olympics.

Hey, It's the NBA!

Michael Jordan, Shaquille O'Neal, and Kevin Garnett would have nowhere to play if not for a key sports merger (a word that means "combined") in 1949. That year, the National Basketball League and the Basketball Association of America joined forces to form the National Basketball Association (NBA). Here are some firsts from NBA history:

First NBA champion: Philadelphia Warriors, 1947 (BAA)

First (and only!) team to win eight straight titles: Boston Celtics, 1959–1966

First NBA Finals MVP, three straight years: Michael Jordan, Chicago, 1991–93 (also 1996 to 1998!)

First Canadian teams: Vancouver Grizzlies and Toronto Raptors, who joined for the 1995–1996 season

First player from China drafted No. 1 overall: The Houston Rockets took 7-foot-6-inch (229-cm) Yao Ming with the first pick in 2002.

Shotmakers

The first basketball players kept both feet on the ground when they shot the ball using a set shot. In the 1930s, Wyoming college player Kenny Sailors changed the game by taking the first jump shots. In 1946, Bob Kurland, a college player, made what some records call the first slam dunk. NBA star George Mikan became the first player to dunk regularly. In the 1960s, Lew Alcindor (later named Kareem Abdul-Jabbar) started shooting the first almost unstoppable skyhooks.

Filling the Bucket

The object of the game, of course, is to score more points than the other team. To fill the bucket. To throw down the rock. To drain. Whatever you call it, scoring rules in hoops. The early games were often very low scoring, however. Teams could hold the ball as long as they wanted before shooting. So, a key first in basketball scoring came on October 30, 1954, when the first game was played using the 24-second shot clock. Beginning with that game, teams had to take a shot within 24 seconds of getting the ball. In that first game using the clock, the Rochester Royals beat the Boston Celtics, 98–95, in an exciting, high-scoring game! The clock idea worked! Here are some other firsts created by basket-filling NBA stars:

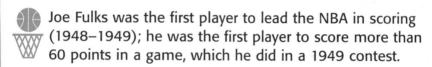

Joe Fulks was the first player to lead the NBA in scoring (1948–1949); he was the first player to score more than 60 points in a game, which he did in a 1949 contest.

On March 2, 1962, Wilt "The Stilt" Chamberlain of the Philadelphia Warriors became the first (and still only!) pro player to score 100 points in a game! He finished that year with 4,029 points, making him the first player to score more than 4,000 points in a season.

Larry Bird was the first player ever to shoot more than 50 percent from the field and more than 90 percent from the free-throw line for his career.

In 1979, the NBA created the three-point shot. Since then, baskets made from behind a line on the court have counted for three points instead of two. Chris Ford of the Boston Celtics made the first NBA three-point shot on October 12, 1979.

March Madness

While many people are fans of pro basketball, other hoops fanatics follow the college game. The national college title game is held in March. The games that lead up to it are known as "March Madness." Here are some college hoops firsts (note: NCAA stands for National Collegiate Athletic Association):

First NCAA champion: University of Oregon, which defeated Ohio State University, 46–33, in 1939

First Final Four: 1939, Oregon, Ohio State, University of Oklahoma, and Villanova University

First back-to-back NCAA champion: Oklahoma A&M, 1945–46

First undefeated champion: The San Francisco Dons, led by center Bill Russell, were 29–0 in 1956.

First champion, seven straight years: UCLA, 1967–73

First NCAA women's champion: Louisiana Tech, which defeated Cheyney State, 76–62, in 1982

First year one school won both men's and women's titles: 2004, University of Connecticut

A Historic Game

The 1966 NCAA Final represented a college basketball landmark: It was the first time in the championships that a single team, Texas Western, started a lineup made up of five African Americans. Only a few years earlier, some teams from the South had refused to play any school that included black players. In the 1966 championship, Texas A&M defeated an all-white Kentucky squad, 72–65.

Women's Hoops

Women began playing basketball not long after its invention in 1891. However, until the 1960s, women's basketball rules were a little different. The court was divided into two or three zones, and players could not move from one zone to another. Originally, this was because it was thought women could not handle too much running—tell that to today's high-flying WNBA stars! Here are some women's basketball firsts:

First college game: In 1896, California played Miss Head's School, a small women's college.

First woman to sign with a men's pro team: Former UCLA star Ann Meyers signed with the Indiana Pacers in 1979, but she did not earn a spot on the roster.

First woman to dunk: Georgeann Wells, West Virginia University, on December 21, 1984

First woman to play in a men's pro league: In 1986, Nancy Lieberman played for the Springfield Fame of the United States Basketball League.

First women's pro league: American Basketball League, 1995

First WNBA champion: The NBA started a women's pro league in 1997. The Houston Comets were the first champs that year.

First woman pro to dunk: Lisa Leslie of the WNBA's Los Angeles Sparks made history on July 30, 2002, when she did a one-handed slam dunk in a game against the Miami Sol.

Kickoff!

Time to huddle up, grab the pigskin, and talk some serious football! First things first: Football did not have one inventor. It evolved from English games such as rugby or soccer. In the late 1800s and early 1900s, the rules of the game changed to speed it up and improve safety. Here are some firsts from the gridiron (which is a nickname for a football field):

First College Football Game

Rutgers University defeated Princeton University, 6–4, at New Brunswick, New Jersey, on November 6, 1869. The game looked more like soccer than modern football—25 players on each team tried to kick a ball across a goal line to score one point.

First Pro Player

All players were unpaid and competed just for the love of the game—until 1892. That's when the Allegheny Athletic Club of Pennsylvania made William (Pudge) Heffelfinger the first pro player by paying him $500—an enormous sum at the time—to play for their club. Salaries have risen slightly (!) since then.

It's About Time!

Believe it or not, football players went without helmets for the first 75 years or so of the sport's history! The first helmets were little more than padded leather caps. The invention of hard plastics in the 1930s and 1940s led to better and safer helmet designs. In 1944, the NFL first made wearing helmets mandatory for all players. In 1948, Fred Gehrke, a Los Angeles Rams running back, painted yellow ram horns on his team's helmets, making the first helmet logo.

Birth of the NFL

In 1920, a group of owners of amateur football teams gathered in an automobile showroom in Canton, Ohio. Standing around amid the shiny new cars, they formed the American Professional Football Association. The legendary player (and former Olympic champ, see page 254) Jim Thorpe was named the league's first president. As the team with the best record, the Akron Pros were the first league champions. Two years later, the league's name was changed to the National Football League (NFL), with Joe Carr serving as the first commissioner.

First Pro Game

The Latrobe YMCA beat the Jeannette Athletic Club, 12–0, on August 31, 1895, in Latrobe, Pennsylvania.

First Forward Passes

The forward pass was first made legal in football in 1906. Passing made the players stay farther apart on the field and helped reduce the large numbers of injuries and even deaths in games.

First Gatorade Dump

New York Giants players Harry Carson and Jim Burt first dumped a bucket of the sticky sports drink on coach Bill Parcells, in 1987.

First Football Spike

New York Giants receiver Homer Jones made the first spike in 1965. Jones scored his first NFL touchdown on a 90-yard pass, and he wanted to celebrate. He was about to heave the ball into the crowd—but it would have cost him a $100 fine. So he threw the ball down as hard as he could. A tradition was born!

Super Bowl Firsts

Beginning in 1966, the NFL champ met the winner of the American Football League (another pro league that had started in 1960) in a game that was first called (take a deep breath) the NFL-AFL World Championship Game. Whew. Thank goodness they changed the name to the Super Bowl in 1969. Today the winners of the NFL's two conferences meet to determine the NFL champ. Here are some Super Bowl firsts:

First Super Bowl: The Green Bay Packers beat Kansas City Chiefs, 35–10, on January 15, 1967, at the L.A. Coliseum.

First touchdown: WR Max McGee, Green Bay, 1967

First Super Bowl MVP: QB Bart Starr, Green Bay, 1967

First three-time MVP: QB Joe Montana, San Francisco 49ers (1982, 1985, 1990)

First wild-card champion: The Oakland Raiders beat the Philadelphia Eagles, 27–10, in 1981.

First indoor Super Bowl: Dallas beat Denver, 27–10, in 1978 in the Louisiana Superdome in New Orleans.

SAY IT FIRST...

first-and-10 When a football team gets the ball, they have four plays, or downs, to gain ten yards. The first play is "first down," which is a team's first chance to move those ten yards. "First-and-10" means that it is first down and ten yards to go for another first down.

Bowl Game Fever!

For many fans, the best kind of football is college football. Hundreds of colleges, small and large, have teams, and current and former students cheer for their schools in packed stadiums. The highlights of most seasons are the bowl games, played after the regular season ends between the top teams in the nation. Here are some bowl game firsts:

YEAR	BOWL GAME	WINNING SCHOOL
1902	*Rose Bowl*	Michigan
1935	*Orange Bowl*	Bucknell
1935	*Sugar Bowl*	Tulane
1937	*Cotton Bowl*	Texas Christian
1946	*Gator Bowl*	Wake Forest
1959	*Liberty Bowl*	Penn State
1968	*Peach Bowl*	Louisiana State

Heisman Trophy

The outstanding college football player of the year is awarded the Heisman Trophy, named for John Heisman, the coach who led Georgia Tech to the national championship in 1917. The **first winner** was Jay Berwanger, halfback, University of Chicago, in 1935. Ohio State running back Archie Griffin was the **first two-time winner** in 1974–75. Charles Woodson of Michigan became the **first defensive player** to win in 1997.

FORE! Tee Time

Golf grew out of games played by shepherds in Scotland and other parts of Britain. They whacked rocks around their pastures with their shepherding staffs. Golf was first organized in Scotland in 1754, when the Society of St. Andrews Golfers set down the rules of the sport. St. Andrews, Scotland, was the site of one of the first golf courses in the world. The first golf course to open in America was Dorset Field Club in Dorset, Vermont, in 1886. The Professional Golfers' Association (PGA) was formed in 1916.

➤➤ In 1962, Jack Nicklaus became the first rookie to win the U.S. Open, the first of his record 20 major championships.

➤➤ In 1963, Arnold Palmer became the first golfer to earn more than $100,000 in a year. In 1958, he became the first to top $1 million in career prize money.

Can't Hold That Tiger

Tiger Woods is the best golfer—and most famous athlete—in the world. By a long shot! Amid his many incredible records, we dug up some amazing firsts for the king of the links (a nickname for a golf course):

YEAR	AGE	FIRST . . .
1991	15	U.S. Junior Amateur Champion under 16
1992	16	Back-to-back Junior Amateur champ (also won in 1993)
1996	20	Winner of three straight U.S. Amateur titles
1997	21	African-American or Asian-American Masters champion ever . . . and first to win title by 12-stroke margin
2000	24	Athlete to win two Sportsman of the Year Awards from *Sports Illustrated* (also won in 1996)
2001	25	Golfer to be champion of all four majors at once

Keeping Score

A score of one under par for a hole is called a "birdie." The term "birdie" was first used in 1898 by Ab Smith while playing the par-four second hole at The Country Club in Atlantic City, New Jersey. When Smith's second shot landed inches from the hole, he said, "That was a bird of a shot." He holed his putt for one under par and such a score became known as a "birdie."

➤➤ In 1977, Al Geiberger became the first PGA Tour player to break 60 for a round, shooting a 59 in the second round of the Memphis Golf Classic at Colonial Country Club.

➤➤ In 2003, Mike Weir became the first left-handed player and the first Canadian to win the prestigious Masters tournament.

The Grand Slam

Golf's greatest tournaments are called the "Grand Slam." In 1930, the great amateur player Bobby Jones was the **first golfer to win the Grand Slam** *when he won the British Amateur and Open championships and the American Amateur and Open championships. (An open championship means that professionals compete with amateurs.) Today, the Grand Slam is made up of the U.S. and British Opens, the Masters, and PGA Championships. Here are the first winners of each event:*

YEAR	EVENT	FIRST WINNER
1860	British Open	Willie Park, Great Britain
1895	U.S. Open	Horace Rawlins, Great Britain
1916	PGA Championship	Jim Barnes, United States
1934	Masters	Horton Smith, United States

Women's Golf

In golf, unlike in some other sports, women have played from the first days of the sport. The first Olympic event for women was, in fact, golf, during the 1900 Paris Olympic Games. Here are some key firsts regarding the ladies on the links:

The Women's Professional Golf Association was first formed in 1944. The Ladies Professional Golf Association (LPGA) replaced it in 1950.

The first U.S. Women's Open in 1946 was won by Patty Berg, who served as the first LPGA president. During the 1959 U.S. Women's Open, Berg became the first woman to get a hole-in-one in official competition!

In 1947, former Olympic track gold medalist Babe Didrikson Zaharias became the first American golfer to win the Women's British Amateur championship.

In 1978, Nancy Lopez became the first woman to win rookie of the year and player of the year honors in the same year. She was also the first to win five tournaments in a row.

Pat Bradley was the first woman to win all four majors (the "Grand Slam") in a career. The women's majors are the U.S. Open, the du Maurier Classic, the Nabisco Championship, and the LPGA Championship.

In 2001, Annika Sorenstam of Sweden became the first woman to shoot a round under 60 when she fired a 59 in Phoenix, Arizona.

In 2002, Michelle Wie became the first 12-year-old (okay, the youngest) woman to play in a pro event; the next year, she was the first 13-year-old to play in a major, the Nabisco Championship. In 2004, she played in her first men's PGA event, the Sony Open.

In 2003, Annika Sorenstam became the first woman since Zaharias in 1945 to compete in a PGA Tour event.

And They're Off!

The earliest record of horse racing dates back to the chariot races in the Roman Empire about 1500 BCE. Below you'll find informaton about modern horse racing and its pioneers (both the horses and the people who rode them!):

The first modern racecourse was established at Newmarket, in England, in 1665. The Jockey Club, the first organization to promote and regulate the sport, was formed around 1750.

Horse racing came to the United States along with the colonists in the late 1600s. British Colonel Richard Nicholls set up the New World's first horse track and staged the first organized races on Long Island, New York.

In 1919, Sir Barton became the first horse to win the Triple Crown, made up of three races—the Kentucky Derby, the Preakness Stakes, and the Belmont Stakes.

In 1970, Diane Crump, riding a horse called Fathom, became the first woman jockey to ride in the Kentucky Derby. She—and Fathom, of course—finished in fifteenth place.

Robyn Smith became the first woman to win a major horse race on March 1, 1973. She rode a horse named North Sea to a first-place finish at Aqueduct, in New York.

7

Ice Hockey Firsts

Hockey, like golf, evolved from several games. Of course, those games were played on ice, not in meadows! Several nations say hockey was born in their lands, including Canada, Russia, and Scandanavian countries. In North America, the first organized league of hockey teams started in Kingston, Ontario, Canada, in 1885. In 1917, the National Hockey League (NHL) began with four teams in Canada. The first NHL team in the United States was the Boston Bruins, who joined in 1924.

The first player to score 50 goals in one season was Maurice "Rocket" Richard, who put 50 "biscuits in the basket" during the 1944–45 season.

In 1960, Gordie "Mr. Hockey" Howe became the first player to score more than 1,000 points in a career. (In hockey, goals and assists each count for one point in a player's scoring totals. Games are decided by goals only.) By playing from 1946–1980, Howe also became the first pro athlete in any sport to play in five different decades.

In 1968–69, Boston's Phil Esposito became the first player to score 100 or more points in a single season, finishing with 126 points.

Drive on the Ice

Ice hockey players are rough on ice–literally! The ice surface gets chewed up by skates, pucks, and sticks. Between periods, a special machine smooths the ice and makes it safe and fast. That machine is the famous Zamboni. The first, named for its inventor Frank Zamboni, appeared during the 1954–55 season at the Boston Garden.

First on the Face

You'd think this would have occurred to goalies *looong* ago, but the first goalie to wear a face mask for protection, Clint Benedict of the Montreal Maroons, didn't wear one until 1930—and then only for one game! It was not until 1959 that Jacques Plante of the Montreal Canadiens became the first goalie to regularly wear a mask—after he was hit in the face by a slap shot. Good call, Jacques.

In 1969–70, Boston's Bobby Orr became the first defenseman to lead the league in scoring, with 120 points. Before then, only forwards were high scorers.

Edmonton's Wayne "The Great One" Gretzky was the first player with 100 assists in one season (109 in 1980–81; he then did it 11 more times!); first with 90 goals in a season (92 in 1981–82); and first with 200 points in one season (212 in 1981–82).

The Stanley Cup

In 1892, Canada's governor general, Lord Stanley of Preston, donated an annual trophy for the best hockey team. His small silver bowl is now called the Stanley Cup. The first winner was the Montreal Athletic Association, an amateur team. The first pro club to win was the Montreal Wanderers in 1910. The first American Stanley Cup champ was the Seattle Metropolitans in 1917. In 1918, the Stanley Cup became part of the new NHL; its first champion was the Toronto Arenas.

Motor Sports

Who drove the first automobile? There are several answers to that one (see page 298). Who drove in the first automobile race? The joke in motor sports is that the first race came on the day someone made the second car! Racing these new machines was a bigger deal for early car makers than selling them to customers. Here are some auto racing firsts:

The first American auto race took place in 1895 in Chicago. The 54-mile (86.9-km) race was won by J. Frank Duryea at an average speed of less than 8 miles (12.8 km) per hour!

In 1903, test driver Barney Oldfield became the first person to drive a mile a minute—that's 60 miles (96 km) per hour.

The first major American race that included international competitors was the Vanderbilt Cup in 1904. A dozen drivers from several countries zoomed for 300 miles (483 km) around a road course on Long Island, New York. The first winner was American George Heath driving a French-made Panhard car.

Indy Firsts

The Indianapolis 500 is one of the world's oldest and most famous races. The first "Indy" 500, in 1911, was won by Ray Harroun, driving a Marmon Wasp at an average speed of 74.6 miles (120.1 km) per hour. In 1925, Peter DePaolo was the winner, and he was the first driver to average more than 100 miles (161 km) per hour. In 1977, Janet Guthrie became the first woman to drive in an Indy 500. In 1992, with an 11th-place finish, Lyn St. James became the first female Indy 500 Rookie of the Year. A. J. Foyt was the first driver to win the Indy 500 four times.

The First King

Richard "The King" Petty is the winningest stock car racer in history. He also racked up more NASCAR firsts in his 33-year career (1959–1992) than any other driver. Among his career highlights:

➤ **First driver with 100 and then 200 career race victories**

➤ **First driver to win the Daytona 500 seven times**

➤ **First driver to win NASCAR championship seven times**

➤ **First driver to win 27 races in one season (1967)**

➤ **First driver to earn more than $1 million in a career**

NASCAR Firsts

The National Association for Stock Car Auto Racing (NASCAR) was formed in 1947 by "Big" Bill France. NASCAR's first race was held in 1948 at Daytona Beach, Florida, and won by Red Byron. Byron was also the first NASCAR season champion, in 1949. In recent years, the popularity of NASCAR racing has skyrocketed and attendance at races has soared. Here are some other significant NASCAR races* and the first winners of each:

YEAR	RACE	TRACK SITE	FIRST WINNER
1949	**Virginia 500**	Martinsville, Virginia	Red Byron
1950	**Southern 500**	Darlington, S. Carolina	Johnny Mantz
1959	**Daytona 500**	Daytona, Florida	Lee Petty
1960	**Coca-Cola 600**	Charlotte, N. Carolina	Joe Lee Johnson
1961	**Food City 500**	Bristol, Tennessee	Jack Smith
1969	**Aaron's 499**	Talladega, Alabama	Richard Brickhouse
1994	**Brickyard 400**	Indianapolis, Indiana	Jeff Gordon

* Race names have changed over the years; listed are their 2004 names.

The Olympic Games

Da-DAH-da-dah-dah-dah-da! Play the fanfare, send in the athletes—the Olympics are here! The Olympics of today follow an ancient Greek tradition. The **first recorded Olympic Games** *occurred in Olympia, Greece, in 776 BCE. The* **first champion** *of that competition was Coroebus, who won a 200-yard (183-m) foot race called a stadion (from which we get the word "stadium"). He was crowned with olive branches. He also wore no clothes, so there are some things the modern Games have improved on!*

Ancient Olympic festivals were held every four years, until 393, when the Olympics were banned by Emperor Theodosius.

In 1896, a Frenchman named Baron Pierre de Coubertin wanted to promote international friendship through athletic competition. He revived the Olympics, setting the **first "modern" Olympics** *in Athens, Greece, their original home. American James B. Connolly won the first event, the "hop, skip, and jump" (now called the triple jump). He didn't win the first gold medal, however—there were no gold medals back then because gold was considered too expensive! Each 1896 winner received a silver medal and crown of olive branches. Here are some other firsts from modern Olympic history:*

Women took part in the Olympics for the first time in 1900, in golf and tennis. Margaret Abbott became the first American female gold medalist when she won the golf event.

In 1908 in London, for the first time, athletes marched into the opening ceremony behind their national flag.

In 1928, the first Olympic flame was lit and burned throughout the Games in Amsterdam, the Netherlands.

➡ After winning a total of five Olympic gold medals, American swimmer Johnny Weissmuller went to Hollywood in 1932 and became the first of four Olympic medalists to play Tarzan in the movies.

➡ In 1936, the first Olympic torch relay was held, carrying the flame from Greece to the site of the Olympics in Berlin, Germany. The 1936 Games were also the first to be shown (at least in part) on TV.

➡ Also in 1936, American sprinter Jesse Owens became the first man to win four gold medals at one Olympics. Owens, an African American, bravely ignored the racist talk of the Nazi government, which led Germany at that time.

➡ In 1960, live color TV broadcasts of the Games from Rome were seen for the first time. Today, the Olympics is one of the most-watched TV events in the world.

➡ In 1968, the Games in Mexico City boasted the first official mascot, a red jaguar that, oddly, did not have a name.

➡ On July 19, 1976, during the Montreal Games, Nadia Comaneci, a 4-foot-11-inch (150-cm), 80-pound (36-kg) 14-year-old from Romania, received the first perfect score of 10 in Olympic gymnastics history.

➡ In 2008, the Summer Olympics will be held for the first time in China, when they are hosted by the city of Beijing.

Track and Field

The ancient Greek Olympics featured many events that are similar to today's track and field events. During the 20th century, American athletes produced many track-and-field highlights and records. Here are some key American firsts from the history of Olympic track and field:

First man to win medals in three straight Olympics: Ray Ewry, 1900, 1904, and 1908

First athlete to win pentathlon and decathlon in the same Olympics: Jim Thorpe, 1912

First teenager to win the Olympic decathlon:
17-year-old Bob Mathias, 1948. He went on to become the first person to win two straight Olympic decathlons.

First person to win the same event four straight times: Al Oerter, discus throw, 1956, 1960, 1964, and 1968

First male 100-meter winner under 10 seconds:
Jim Hines, 1968

First female 100-meter winner under 11 seconds:
Evelyn Ashford, 1984

First women's marathon winner: Joan Benoit, 1984

First man to win 200- and 400-meter runs:
Michael Johnson, 1996

Winter Olympics

The winter wonders of the world were jealous. What about our sports? they said. The first Winter Olympic Games were held in 1924, in Chamonix, France. The first Winter Games held in the United States were at Lake Placid, New York, in 1932. Now let's bundle up for some Winter Games firsts:

❄ Eddie Eagan of the U.S. was the first athlete to win gold medals in both the Summer and Winter Olympics. He won a gold in boxing in 1920 and a gold in the four-man bobsled event at the 1932 Winter Games.

❄ In 1948, Dick Button won the first U.S. Olympic figure skating gold medal at the St. Mortiz Games in Switzerland, wowing the judges with the first double axel ever performed in competition. This was also the first Olympics with Alpine skiing competitions.

❄ The first U.S. woman to win a Winter Olympics gold medal was Tenley Albright of Newton Center, Massachusetts, who captured the figure skating title in 1956.

❄ In 1992, Bonnie Blair won the gold medal in the 500-meter speed skating event in Albertville, France, becoming the first American woman to win gold medals in consecutive Winter Olympics.

❄ In 1984, in the Alpine slalom skiing competition, Phil and Steve Mahre of the U.S. became the first brothers to finish first and second in an Olympic event.

❄ America's Donna Weinbrecht won the first gold medal in the new women's moguls competition in 1992. Mogul skiers perform jumps with names like daffies, kosaks, zudniks, and helicopters.

Goooooaaallll!

Soccer (or football, as it is known around the world) is the world's most popular sport—by far! But it has only become that popular in a little more than a century. Read on to find out more about soccer history:

The world's first soccer team, the Sheffield Football Club, was formed in England, in 1857.

In 1904, the Fédération Internationale de Football Association (FIFA) was formed. FIFA is the organization that runs soccer all over the world. By 1913, the United States had been accepted as a member of FIFA.

The World Cup is a major soccer tournament held every four years to determine the best national team in the world. The first winner was Uruguay in 1930. The first World Cup held in the United States was in 1994.

The United States won the first Women's World Cup in 1991. America's Carin Gabarra was named the first winner of that tournament's most outstanding player award.

The American Youth Soccer Organization (AYSO) was first formed in California in 1964.

The Atlanta Chiefs were the first champions of the North American Soccer League (which was America's first pro outdoor soccer league) in 1968.

In 1969, playing with the Santos club in Brazil, the incredible Pelé became the first player to score more than 1,000 career goals.

The first champion of Major League Soccer, a pro league that first played in 1996, was D.C. United.

Tennis Firsts

Tennis began in the 1500s in France as court tennis, an indoor game. In 1873, Major Clopton Wingfield of England moved the game outside and played it on grass. Lawn tennis, as the sport was soon called, quickly became popular. By the late 1870s, there were tennis clubs all over the world.

The first organized tournament was held in 1877 at the All England Croquet and Lawn Tennis Club, the site of today's Wimbledon championships. Spencer W. Gore was the first winner. The first ladies' final was contested seven years later. That year, in the first major tournament battle between siblings, Maud Watson beat her sister Lilian.

Grand Slam Firsts

A tennis player who wins, in the same year, all four of these important tournaments—the Australian, U.S., and French Opens, and Wimbledon—is said to have won the "Grand Slam."

In 1938, American Don Budge became the first player to capture the Grand Slam. In 1951, American Maureen Connolly became the first woman to win it.

Steffi Graf of Germany won a "golden" Grand Slam in 1988. After winning all four majors, she became the first to also win an Olympic gold medal in tennis in the same year.

Here are the first winners of the Grand Slam tournaments:

Wimbledon

MEN	1877	Spencer W. Gore
WOMEN	1884	Maud Watson

U.S. Open

MEN	1881	Richard D. Sears
WOMEN	1887	Ellen Hansell

Australian Open

MEN	1905	Rodney Heath
WOMEN	1922	Margaret Molesworth

French Open

MEN	1925	René Lacoste
WOMEN	1925	Suzanne Lenglen

257

Like, Firsts, Dude!

Skateboarders started out just swapping tricks with their friends and hangin' with their buds, right? (See page 81.) But, yo, the best way to get some street cred was to win a competition. Here are some firsts from the sport of skateboarding—as opposed to the art!

✔ The first contest in skateboarding history was held at the Pier Avenue Junior School in Hermosa, California, in 1963. That same year, Gary Swanson skated inside an empty pool in his Santa Monica backyard, inventing the vert style of skating.

✔ Curved plywood ramps designed for skateboarding were first used in 1975, in Melbourne Beach, Florida. Port Orange, Florida, was the site of the first skateboard park, Skatboard City, which opened in 1976. They thought it would be cool to misspell the name on purpose. Later that year, the first smooth concrete skatepark opened in Carlsbad, California.

✔ The first X Games skateboarding results, from the first event in Rhode Island in 1995:

Vert: Tony Hawk   **Street:** Chris Senn

Best Trick: Jamie Thomas   **High Air:** Danny Way

✔ The ollie (a move skaters use to get all four wheels of the board off the ground at once) was created in 1978 by Alan Gelfand, whose nickname was . . . Ollie!

✔ Tony Hawk should have "first" as part of his name. He was the first to do so many tricks, it's just sick! Among them are the air walk (1983), the Madonna (1984), the 720 aerial (1985), and the gravity-defying 900 (1999).

✔ In 1990, Cara-Beth Burnside was the first woman to become a professional skateboarder.

First in Shred!

Skaters with nothing to do in the cold, snowy winter months were saved by a . . . snurfer? Skateboard whizzes were among the first to flock to the new sport of snowboarding. It started out with a toy called the Snurfer, which was similar to a water ski with a rope on the front end. It was made by the Brunswick Sporting Goods Company in the 1960s. In the 1970s, a man named Jake Burton, who had been given a Snurfer when he was a kid, invented the first snowboard by making his Snurfer wider and adding two skegs (fins) on the bottom. By the late 1970s, snowboarding had taken off. Like skateboarding, snowboarding is as much about fun and freedom as about winning—but winning's nice, too!

U.S. Snowboarding Championships

Here are the winners from the first pro championship in 1994:

Slalom — MEN: Anton Pogue; WOMEN: Stacia Hookman

Giant Slalom — MEN: Steve Persons; WOMEN: Elka Barnes

Freestyle — MEN: Ross Powers; WOMEN: Sabrina Sadeghi

The Olympics

Snowboarding became an Olympic-medal sport for the first time in 1998 in Nagano, Japan. Here are the first gold medal winners:

Giant Slalom — MEN: Ross Rebagliati, Canada
WOMEN: Karine Ruby, France

Halfpipe — MEN: Gian Simmen, Switzerland
WOMEN: Nicola Thost, Germany

First Plays . . .

We'll wrap up our sport-by-sport breakdown of firsts with this list of things that you see first at different sporting events. You can't have sports firsts without first starting to play the games (or run the races). Here is a list of things that happen first in sports:

SPORT	FIRST THING
Basketball	tip-off
Boxing	single bell ring
Football, soccer, rugby	kickoff
Motor sports	green flag/light
Horse racing	ringing bell
Golf	tee shot
Hockey	face-off
Running races	starter's pistol
Swimming races	electronic tone
Tennis	first serve

SAY IT FIRST...

first string In team sports, a group of athletes starts each contest. These players are often referred to as the "first team" or "first string," as in a string of players running out onto the field first.

CHAPTER 12

Technology

Beep, buzz, zap, click, dot-com, :-) . . . all the stuff that makes our wired world hum had to start somewhere. In this chapter, read about firsts in technologies new and old, and how some things you thought were brand-new have been around for quite a while!

Light Us Up!

The first light on Earth? That's easy. The Sun! Next page. Oh, you want more? Okay, we've got some other light "firsts." From fire to electricity, humans have always been looking for ways to capture the Sun's energy—without all that sizzling heat, of course. Slip on your shades and read on!

First Matches

Fire was created in prehistoric times, of course, first probably by lightning and later by cavepeople rubbing sticks and flints together. Other than that, humans could not "create" fire until phosphorus, a substance that glows in the dark, was discovered in 1669. In 1680, Robert Boyle, an Irish-English chemist, found that he could create a fire by rubbing a piece of wood he had coated with sulfur against a piece of paper he had coated with phosphorus. In 1827, English scientist John Walker made the first matches that could be struck just about anywhere to light.

First Lightbulb

Here's a good one to surprise your teacher with: Thomas Edison did *not* invent the lightbulb! He did, however, make the first useful one. Joseph Swan of England made the first lightbulb in 1878. Lightbulbs make light by using electricity to heat a thin strip of material (called a filament) until it gets hot enough to glow. Swan's filament, made from cotton fiber, produced a faint glow in a glass tube for 14 hours. In October 1879, Edison kept his filament burning in a glass bulb for 40 hours. Over the next two years, Edison tested thousands of different filaments in search of the longest-lasting one. He finally found his answer by the end of 1880, when he produced a bamboo-filament bulb that glowed for 1,200 hours!

Huge improvements have since been made to lightbulbs. By 1910, William Coolidge of the General Electric company had discovered that a filament made of tungsten could glow for 10,000 hours. In 1991, the Philips Corporation introduced a bulb that could last 60,000 hours.

First Neon Light

The word "neon" comes from the Greek *neos*, meaning "the new gas." In 1902, French inventor Georges Claude was the first person to apply an electrical charge to a sealed tube of neon gas to create a lamp. You could even say it glowed! (Sorry.) Claude introduced neon gas signs to the United States in 1923, on a car dealership in Los Angeles and a theater in New York City.

First Fluorescent Light

A fluorescent ("glowing") light works when electricity heats mercury vapors. In 1901, American scientist Peter Hewitt made the first mercury vapor lamp using a glass tube. Electric current passing through the mercury gas vapor in the tube made it glow. In 1934, the General Electric Company switched the gas to argon to create today's fluorescent lights.

Spotlight on Flashlights

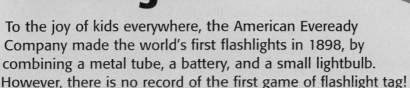

To the joy of kids everywhere, the American Eveready Company made the world's first flashlights in 1898, by combining a metal tube, a battery, and a small lightbulb. However, there is no record of the first game of flashlight tag!

That Man Edison

With more than 1,000 patents to his name, Thomas Alva Edison is surely America's greatest inventor, and thus America's greatest maker of firsts. His most famous firsts—the phonograph, a practical electric lightbulb, an electric generating system, the moving picture camera (see page 37), and a sound-recording machine (page 61)—helped create enormous industries and improve people's lives all over the world.

Edison was not always the first to try to make these machines, but he was the first to make them practical. For example, he was not the first person to experiment with electric light. But he built the first power plants that could deliver the electricity to power electric lights into people's homes at an affordable rate. In this way, he was a true visionary.

Edison received his first patent in 1869 for a vote counter, but found no buyers for it. Edison vowed never again to invent something unless he was sure to make money. His motto of "inventions to order" led him to manufacture improved telegraph machines (see page 266) over the next several years. He opened a laboratory in Menlo Park, New Jersey, in 1876.

The laboratory Edison created was a remarkable invention in itself. It was like an invention factory. At Menlo Park, Edison employed brilliant scientists and engineers to create bold new ideas. Electricians, ironworkers, and carpenters helped turn the ideas into reality. Then other employees worked to submit the invention for a patent.

Nearly deaf in both ears, Edison could focus and concentrate on work with an amazing intensity. Even failure did not deter his enthusiasm. When a fellow scientist expressed frustration after efforts to create a superior battery had resulted in 8,000 failures, Edison refused to give up, saying, "Well, at least we know 8,000 things that don't work!"

That was Edison's genius, the knowledge that even a lack of progress is a form of progress. After all, it was Edison who first said, "Genius is 1 percent inspiration and 99 percent perspiration." In other words, you have to work very hard to change a great idea into something useful. Edison did that better and more often than anyone else.

Beats Yelling!

For thousands of years, the only way people communicated was by talking or writing. That's right, folks, no e-mail! No telephones, no pagers, no beepers, no radios. However, the first forms of communication other than speaking or writing were telegraphs, a word that in Greek means "distance writing." Telegraphs are a way to communicate by using coded signals to represent letters of the alphabet. Here are some key firsts in telegraph history:

1793 Claude Chappe of France used flags to represent letters. The flags sat atop a series of towers that could be viewed with a telescope.

1800 The first flag telegraph system in the United States was built by Jonathan Grout. It used flags to send information between ships traveling between Martha's Vineyard and Boston, Massachusetts. It would take 10 minutes to send and receive an answer over this 90-mile (145-km) distance.

1837 William Cooke and Charles Wheatstone of Great Britain patented a quicker electric telegraph by using an electromagnet to send and receive electric signals over long distances. Their telegraph transmitted information over 26 wires—one for each letter of the alphabet.

1838 American inventor Samuel Morse created a telegraph system with just one wire between the sender and receiver. The message was transmitted by an alphabet code that uses short and long electrical pulses, known as dots and dashes. This code is known as Morse code (see the box). Morse received the first Morse code telegram, sent by his partner, Alfred Vail, in January 1838.

Morse code

Morse code is an electronic alphabet that was patented in 1840 (U.S. Patent No. 1,647). Using the Morse code alphabet, this is how you'd spell "Book of Firsts":

(B) – • • • **(O)** – – – **(O)** – – – **(K)** – • –

(O) – – – **(F)** • • – •

(F) • • – • **(I)** • • **(R)** • – • **(S)** • • • **(T)** – **(S)** • • •

1840 Vail invented the telegraph key, which clacked loudly in response to the electric pulses, so that the operator could hear the code.

1844 The first telegraph line between cities was completed from Baltimore, Maryland, to Washington, D.C. The first message Morse sent, on May 24, was a phrase from the Bible: "What hath God wrought?" Morse opened the first telegraph station in Washington, D.C., that year.

1851 The Western Union company was founded to build the first telegraph line across the country, mainly alongside railroad tracks. The line reached California ten years later. The first transcontinental message, congratulating everyone on the feat, was sent by President Abraham Lincoln.

1933 Western Union introduced the singing telegram. Instead of a messenger dropping off a printout of your message, the messenger would sing it to the recipient!

Note: *By this time, telegraphs were going out of style as telephones became a better and faster means of communicating (see page 268).*

It's for You

Okay, telegraphs were pretty cool: You read a message to an operator, the operator typed it in code, it zinged over wires, and someone at the other end decoded it and read it to the person you were writing to. Actually, when you put it like that, there had to be a better way. There was: the telephone. Few inventions in modern history have been as successful, as important, or as wide-ranging as the telephone. Here are some important firsts in the development of telephones:

Inventor Wars!

In 1875, a pair of American inventors battled for the right to say they had "invented" the telephone. Elisha Gray had made the first "tin-can" telephone, connecting two cans by wire so that sound travels over the wire from can to can. (It still works— try it out!)

Meanwhile, Alexander Graham Bell, a speech teacher for the deaf in Boston, Massachusetts, made a similar device, but his used electricity.

Bell received the first patent for a telephone (Patent No. 174,465), but Gray argued that he had invented it, all the way to the U.S. Supreme Court, where he lost.

No Busy Signals!

The first telephone message was sent on March 10, 1876, when Bell's voice became the first to be transmitted. Bell spoke into his cone-shaped telephone and

said to his assistant, Thomas Watson, who was in the next room: "Mr. Watson, come here, I want you." Later that year, Bell and Watson had a conversation over a two-mile (3.2-km) long wire.

No One to Call

In April 1877, the first private telephone was installed in the office of Charles Williams, Jr., of Boston, Massachusetts. In 1878, Bell's assistant, Watson, had the bright idea of putting a bell at each end of the phone lines so that a person would know when someone was calling!

Lots of People to Call

Phone use spread with the installation of telephone wires. The first neighborhood to have phones installed together was New Haven, Connecticut, in 1878. By March 1884, the first intercity link was put into service between New York and Boston. Service between New York and Chicago started in 1892, and by 1912, the network extended to Denver, Colorado.

Going Long Distance

Unfortunately, early telephone signals weakened as the lines grew longer. In 1906, Lee De Forest invented an amplifier that made greater distances possible. In January 1915, the first call across the United States was made between Bell in New York and Watson in San Francisco. Bell repeated the same message— "Mr. Watson, come here, I want you"—that he first used in 1876. Of course, Watson didn't make the trip this time!

To England . . . and Beyond!

In 1915, the first transatlantic telephone call was made from Virginia to Paris, France, using a radio transmitter on the Eiffel Tower. In 1927, the first commercial telephone service was opened between New York and London, England. It spread quickly to the rest of the world over the coming years.

Hooked on Phones

Telephones are such a huge part of our lives, it's hard to believe that they weren't always around. Here are some other phone firsts you might not have thought about!

Got Change?

The first public pay telephone was installed in the lobby of the Hartford Bank of Connecticut in 1889.

They Didn't Have Buttons?!

Early telephone users had to place all their calls through an operator, who would dial the number for them. In 1891, Almon B. Strowger, tired of operators connecting him to wrong numbers, patented the first rotary dial telephone. In 1941, push-button dialing was first tested on phones, but it didn't come into wide use for more than 20 years.

Basic Black

Early telephones were large, bulky objects mounted on a wall. In 1910, the Western Electric Company made the first upright desk phone. The user spoke into a cone atop a small stick while holding a wire-connected receiver to their ear. The invention of phone jacks in the 1960s meant that phones could be made in different shapes, sizes, and colors.

At the Beep . . .

The first telephone answering machine was sold by the Ohio Bell Telephone Company in 1951. Up to 20 30-second messages could be recorded on a magnetic cylinder, which could be cleaned and used again.

Cell Phone Firsts

Raise your hand if you thought cell phones have been around forever. Well, for most of you, that's true, but for us old geezers, they're still pretty new and exciting technology. A cellular phone is a type of wireless communication. The name "cellular" comes from the tall towers that create a system of transfer stations. The towers divide a service area into multiple "cells." Cellular calls are transferred from tower to tower as the user travels from cell to cell.

First cell phone call: Though it looked like a brick and weighed 30 pounds (13.6 kg), the first phone you could use without wires was a breakthrough. Dr. Martin Cooper of Motorola invented it in 1973 and used it to make the first call on a portable phone to his rival, Joel Engel of Bell Laboratories. Technology helped shrink Cooper's brick down to the tiny cell phones we enjoy today.

First cell phone system: AT&T and Bell Labs invented the first cellular telephone system in 1977, an experimental one in Washington, D.C. The world's first commercial cell service was made available in Tokyo, Japan, in 1979.

First international cell phone system: The Finnish company Nokia put cell phones in cars in the first network that could be used to call other countries.

First cell phone system in America: America's first cellular system went into operation in Chicago, Illinois, in 1983.

First Web-enabled cell phone: The NeoPoint 1000, which debuted in 1998, first allowed users access to the Internet.

Radio, Radio

Hop in the car, flip on the radio, right? Not always. Radio has only been around for a little more than a century. Here are some of the firsts on radio's way into cars and headphones around the world:

First radio transmissions: In 1895, Guglielmo Marconi zapped radio signals across his family's home in Bologna, Italy. The following year, Marconi moved to England, where he transmitted and received Morse code signals over a 1.2-mile (2-km) distance. In 1900, Marconi formed the Marconi Wireless Telegraph (an early name for radio) Company and got the world's first radio patent. He wasn't sending voices yet, just electronic signals like Morse's telegraph . . . but without wires.

First radio signals sent across Atlantic: In 1901, Marconi sent a message from England to Newfoundland.

First voice transmission: In 1906, American Reginald Fessenden transmitted the first human voices over the radio.

First radio station: In 1920, Station 8MK of Detroit began daily broadcasts. The station's call letters (its name) were later changed to WWJ.

Phony Marconi?

Marconi gets all the credit, but should he? In 1893, Nikola Tesla of Croatia demonstrated a radio transmission in St. Louis. Yet in 1909, Marconi won the Nobel Prize for inventing radio. However, in 1943—a few months after Tesla's death—the U.S. Supreme Court revoked Marconi's patent and granted Tesla radio Patent No. 645,576. So while Marconi was the first to come up with ways to use the technology, it was Tesla who was really the first to create radio signals.

The First SOS

Marconi promoted the use of radio as a way to communicate with ships at sea. The importance of radio for safety at sea was dramatized on the foggy night of January 22–23, 1909, when the ship *Florida* rammed the ocean liner *Republic* off the coast of Massachusetts. Of the nearly 2,000 people aboard both ships, only six lives were lost, thanks to the distress signal sent by the *Republic's* radio operator and heard by a nearby rescue ship.

First car radio: Finally, something to do while you're driving! The first car radio was invented in 1929 by Paul Galvin of Chicago. The radio was nearly the size of a large mailbox, and the speaker was hidden under the driver's feet.

First FM station: FM (frequency modulation) radio was the invention of Edwin Armstrong, an electrical engineer at Columbia University in New York City, in 1933. FM is a superior system to AM (amplitude modulation, if you must know) because it is static-free and the signal is less affected by weather conditions, such as wind, lightning, and thunderstorms (remember, radio signals are whizzing through the air all around you!). In 1939, WDRC in Connecticut became the first FM station.

First transistor radio: Tiny transistors that carry power and pick up radio signals revolutionized radios. Radios could now be made much smaller and less expensively. The first transistor radio to be made was the Regency, in 1953. Sony introduced the first pocket-sized transistor radio in 1960.

Smile! Photo Firsts

Thanks to a chemical reaction, we have modern photography. In the early 1800s, people figured out how to preserve images on silver-coated paper or plates using light. The word "photography," first used in 1839 to describe this process, comes from Greek words meaning "writing with light."

World's First Photograph

In 1826, French printmaker Joseph-Nicephore Niepce used the silver method to capture an image on a pewter plate. It was a view of the rooftops from a window outside his house in Gras, France. It took eight hours for the silver to make the picture.

First "Convenient" Photographs

Photography was made accessible to the public in 1839; Frenchman Louis Daguerre created a process that cut the exposure time to about six minutes. He called his process the daguerreotype (gee, wonder where he got the name?). People lined up to preserve their images. By 1850, there were more than 70 daguerreotype portrait studios in New York City alone.

First Class Picture

Okay, you've all been in one. How many of you made a funny face? The first class photo in America was of a 30th reunion class at Yale University in 1840. Close readers of our book have already met the photographer: Samuel Morse, the telegraph guy.

First Photo Prints

Daguerreotypes and other photographs could not be reproduced. Each was a one-and-only original. In 1844, English scientist William Talbot invented a method for making a paper

negative from which multiple prints of the same photo could be made.

First Handheld Camera

Cameras were large, bulky things until the Kodak No. 1 model was sold in 1888 by George Eastman of Rochester, New York. Anyone could now take pictures, send the roll off to be processed, and receive the prints by mail. The Eastman Kodak Company's motto was, "You press the button, we do the rest."

First Stop-Action Photography

Thanks to Harold Edgerton, people could "freeze" action for the first time. In 1927, he created a way to make the flash of a strobe light match the opening of a camera shutter. Previously unimaginable images, such as the splash of a single water droplet, were now possible to capture on film.

First Color Film

Kodachrome was developed by Leopold Godowsky and Leopold Mannes at the Eastman Kodak Company in 1935.

First Instant Camera

The Polaroid camera, invented by Dr. Edwin Land in 1947, used photographic paper covered with chemicals. You simply took the picture, waited about a minute, and then peeled apart the paper to reveal a picture.

First Digital Camera

The Sony Corporation introduced the Mavica in 1981 as a "revolutionary video still camera." This first filmless camera recorded and stored 50 images on a two-inch (5-cm) magnetic disk.

Beam Us Up

Telegraph signals racing along wires, radio waves zooming all around us, telephone calls bouncing around like electronic Ping-Pong balls! All those communications tools are forms of energy. Scientists have harnessed other forms of energy to work for humanity in some pretty cool ways. From laser beams to touch screens, here are some fab energy facts:

Laser, Not Phaser

You've probably seen laser beams. These red, glowing lights are used in everything from bar code readers to automatic doors to those laser-tag games. They are also used in hundreds of ways by businesses and industries. Before there were lasers, there were masers. Both are devices that amplify, or strengthen, types of energy. Masers ramp up microwaves; lasers make light more powerful and focused. In fact, laser stands for "light amplification by stimulated emission of radiation." (The "m" in maser is for "microwave.") In 1959, Charles Townes and Arthur Schawlow were granted a patent for the maser, which was used by space researchers to amplify radio signals beyond Earth's atmosphere.

The next year, Gordon Gould, a student of Townes at Columbia University, was the first person to use the word "laser." The first operating laser was developed by Theodore Maiman in 1960.

First Fiber Optics

Lasers led to another invention you might have seen: fiber optics. Many of the high-tech devices you see in your home, at school, or in businesses carry these glass fibers—some as thin as a human hair! Lasers travel through them, transmitting energy and light—and information. Researchers at Corning Glass invented fiber-optic wire in 1970. One strand of fiber-optic cable can carry 65,000 times more information than copper wire.

Touch and Go

Touch-screen technology began with the first "touch sensor," called the Elograph, developed and patented by Dr. Sam Hurst of the University of Kentucky Research Foundation in 1971. The Elograph was not transparent like the touch-screen technology in use today, but it enabled users to navigate a computer system by touching the screen. In 1977, Hurst introduced the touch screens most familiar to us now, such as those used to operate an ATM.

Atomic Energy

One of the most powerful forms of energy has been around since the beginning of the universe—but it was not until 1942 that we learned to harness it. When an atom splits, enormous energy is released. In 1942, scientist Enrico Fermi, using ideas developed by the physicist Albert Einstein, was the first to split an atom, creating atomic energy (a similar type is called nuclear energy). Though first used to make bombs in 1945, this energy was used in a more positive way: The first commercial nuclear-power plant began generating electricity in Shippingport, Pennsylvania, in 1959.

Computers

You know them, you love them, you can't live without them. Whether you spend all your computer time gaming or surfing the Net, or whether you actually do all your homework on it, computers have become a part of life that most people can't do without. You see them in use every day: Computers help control traffic lights, they help run big electricity systems, they mail checks to people from banks and the government . . . they're everywhere! But not too long ago, they didn't exist. From the first computers (which were the size of your classroom) to the first mouse to the first e-mail, these next few pages will try to fill you in on computer firsts. Then you can go back to playing Donkey Kong or whatever. . . .

The ***first electronic computer*** was called the Electronic Numerical Integrator and Computer, or ENIAC. It was designed by Dr. Presper Eckert and Dr. John Mauchly and first demonstrated in February 1946 in Aberdeen, Maryland. The ENIAC could perform 5,000 additions and 300 multiplications per second. The next best machine of the day could do one multiplication per second. The ENIAC weighed 30 tons (27,216 kg) and filled a room the size of a swimming pool! The use of more than 17,000 vacuum tubes (which looked like small lightbulbs) instead of relay switches gave the ENIAC its speed, but it could take technicians weeks to reprogram it between uses.

In 1951, Eckert and Mauchly introduced the ***first business computer***, called the Universal Automatic Computer or UNIVAC. This computer stored data on magnetic tape and could remember 1,000 different numbers. Besides addition and multiplication, the

UNIVAC could also divide, subtract, and figure out square roots and cube roots. The Remington Rand Corporation, the **first American computer maker**, sold 46 UNIVAC computers. The original UNIVAC is now housed at the Smithsonian Institute in Washington, D.C.

Remington Rand also made the **first high-speed computer printer**, for use with the UNIVAC, in 1951.

The **first programming language** was FORTRAN, short for "formula translation." It was the work of an IBM engineer named John Backus, who in 1957 introduced FORTRAN to read digital code. FORTRAN is still used today for a variety of programming, from video games to air traffic control.

The **first supercomputer** was the CRAY-1 computer. Invented by Seymour Cray and introduced in 1976, this machine could perform more than 100 million arithmetic operations per second. That would be handy for your next math test, huh?

The **first computer bug** was a real bug—a moth, to be exact. The moth flew into the circuit board of the Mark II computer at Harvard University in 1945. The bug, which famed computer pioneer Admiral Grace Hopper removed with tweezers, was preserved and can be seen at the Naval Museum in Dahlgren, Virginia. Because of this incident, a problem with a computer or a program is called a "bug." Better than "computer moth," I guess!

To the Desktop!

Computers were used by businesses, governments, scientists, and others before "regular" folks got their hands on them. And we're not letting go! Here are the key firsts in the development of what are called "personal" computers:

First Personal Computer

The Altair 8800 was introduced on the January 1975 cover of *Popular Electronics* magazine. It was developed by Edward Roberts of Micro Instrumentation and Telemetry Systems (MITS), in Albuquerque, New Mexico. The Altair 8800 cost $400 and was named after a planet from the *Star Trek* television series. One catch: You had to build it yourself!

First PC Programming Language

The first programming language for student programmers was BASIC, which stands for Beginner's All-purpose Symbolic Instruction Code. BASIC was written in 1963 by two Dartmouth College math professors, John Kemeny and Tom Kurtz, who wanted to teach students a simple computer programming language. The importance of BASIC as a programming language for personal computers was clear by 1975, when Microsoft founders Paul Allen and Bill Gates wrote a version of BASIC for the Altair personal computer. (This software became the first product ever sold by Microsoft.)

First Apple Computer

The first Apple computer, called the Apple I, was released on April Fools' Day, 1976, by company founders Steve Wozniak and

Steve Jobs. The Apple I was the first single circuit board computer. The first personal computer with color graphics was the Apple II, released the following year.

First IBM PC

On August 12, 1981, IBM released its first computer for home use, called the IBM PC. The "PC" stood for "personal computer." The personal computing age had begun.

First Windows Operating System

Microsoft shipped Windows 1.0 on November 20, 1985. Windows now runs more PCs than any other software.

First Portable Computer

Apple Computer released the first Macintosh Portable in September 1989, which evolved into the Powerbook laptop computer. In October 1992, IBM released its first laptop computer, the ThinkPad 700.

First Computer Game!

Here's the one you've all been waiting for! The first interactive computer game with graphics was Spacewar!, an interstellar-combat game written by graduate students at the Massachusetts Institute of Technology, and first demonstrated to the public in 1962. That's not a typo . . . 1962! (For more gaming firsts, see page 282.)

Computer and Video

Computer and video games have a much longer history than you might think. No, your grandparents didn't play Donkey Kong and your parents probably still don't know your Game Boy from your Xbox, but video games have still been around for a while. From the earliest basic games to the newest high-end, 3-D Internet games, here are some firsts from the world of electronic gaming:

1952 First computer game: Tic-Tac-Toe, created by British computer scientist A. S. Douglas, but usable only on his computer

1958 First video game: Tennis for Two, played on a scientific monitor called an oscilloscope and invented by William Higinbotham of Britain

1962 First computer game usable on many computers: Spacewar!, created by Steve Russell at Massachusetts Institute of Technology

1967 First video game made for use on a TV: Chase, invented by Ralph Baer

1971 First arcade video game: Computer Space,

Game Day •••••••••

Here's the debut year of some famous video games:

Pac-Man	1980	Madden NFL	1989
Asteroids	1980	Super Mario Brothers	1990
Donkey Kong	1981	Sonic the Hedgehog	1991
Frogger	1981	Harry Potter and the	
Ms. Pac-Man	1982	Sorcerer's Stone	2001
Tetris	1989	Spider-Man 2	2004

Games

created by Nolan Bushnell and Ted Dabney and based on Russell's game

1972 First home video game system: Odyssey, released by Magnavox, featured 12 different games, but was not widely used

1972 First home video game: Pong, created by Bushnell. Pong was the first video game to be widely popular. In addition to playing it at home, people played on consoles installed everywhere from restaurants to waiting rooms. The first Pong was put in Andy's Capps, a restaurant in Sunnyvale, California, in 1972.

1977 First release of Atari 2600, the first home game cartridge system to enjoy wide popularity

1977 First Space Invaders game released; this game is the first to feature a "high score" display

1984 First sale of Sega system

1985 First sale of Nintendo Entertainment System

1989 First sale of Nintendo Game Boy

1993 First multiplayer, multicomputer game, Doom, is released.

1993 First CD-only game system, 3DO, debuted.

1994 First release of Sony PlayStation

1996 First three-dimensional multiplayer Internet game: Quake

2000 First sale of Sony PlayStation 2

2001 First sale of Microsoft Xbox

Computer Stuff

What's a computer system without lots of other gear and gadgets? A boring one, that's what. Here are some firsts about those other machines that we use with computers.

The **first commercial modem**, called the Bell 103, was made by American Telephone & Telegraph (AT&T) in 1962. A modem (trivia time: that word stands for modulator/demodulator) is a device that sends and receives data between two computers. It accomplishes this by converting digital information to an analog signal, a type of signal that can be transmitted to another computer over a telephone line. The first modems could transmit only 300 bits per second. Over the next 30 years, as technology improved, the speed with which modems transmitted data skyrocketed, too. In 1996, Dr. Brent Townshend unveiled the first 56K (56,000 bits per second) high-speed modem.

The **first computer mouse** was invented by Douglas Engelbart of the Palo Alto (Calif.) Research Center, in 1968. Originally called an "X-Y Position Indicator" (aren't you glad they came up with "mouse"?), the device controlled the movement of the cursor on the display screen, freeing the user's hands from the keyboard. The breakthrough technology also enabled people to develop "point and click" applications. Where did the name "mouse" come from? If you've seen one (that's not wireless), you know.

It's a little thing with a long tail (the wire). Plus, it moves across a surface much like a mouse scurrying across the floor. The Xerox Corporation began manufacturing the first mouses (mice?) in the early 1970s.

The **first computer storage disks** were developed by a team of research engineers led by Alan Shugart at International Business Machines (IBM). They were introduced in 1971 as "memory disks." These 8-inch (203-mm) plastic disks were the first forms of digital information storage. The nickname "floppy" came from the disk's flexibility. Shugart developed a smaller 5¼-inch (133-mm) diskette for Wang Laboratories in 1976. In 1981, Sony introduced the first 3½-inch (89-mm) disk that we use today.

The **first laser printers** developed by Xerox were demonstrated in 1971. To make them, Xerox added a laser beam to existing Xerox copier technology. In 1992, Hewlett-Packard released the LaserJet 4 printer, the first home laser printer.

The **first inkjet printer** was invented in 1976, but did not become popular for home use until 1988, when Hewlett-Packard released the DeskJet inkjet printer.

The **first PDAs**, or Personal Digital Assistants, were released in 1993 by several companies. PDAs are pen-based, handheld computers.

Birth of the Net

To trace the beginning of the Internet, start with Sputnik, the first satellite sent into orbit. In response to this move by the Soviet Union, the United States started the Advanced Research Projects Agency, or ARPA. Looking for a way to connect their computers in a secure network, ARPA developed a program called ARPANET in 1969. This military network soon became widely used by civilians and was renamed the Internet.

The ***first computer connections of the ARPANET*** were at UCLA, Stanford Research Institute (SRI), the University of California at Santa Barbara, and the University of Utah. The ***first exchange of information*** by this new network occurred in 1969 between a computer at UCLA and one at SRI.

The ***first cross-country link*** of the ARPANET was between UCLA and Massachusetts Institute of Technology in 1970.

In 1974, a new ARPANET spin-off, the Telenet, made these connections ***available to the public for the first time;*** previously, only schools and governments could use the network. As it grew, it was renamed the Internet in 1982.

The First Chat Room

The growing popularity of personal computers in the late 1970s brought a huge number of people to the newfangled network. Besides sending e-mail (see page 287), folks took part in online discussion groups. The first was Usenet, which began in 1979. Usenet was a series of electronic bulletin boards where people could post messages and others would reply. It was this spirit of information sharing that made it possible for the Internet to grow so quickly in both technology and popularity. Anyone with a computer and a modem could not only contribute to the Net, but they could come up with ways to make it better for everyone. More than ever before, the world became a connected place.

TheFirst@E-mail

To businesspeople, families, students, government agencies—and, yes, spammers—e-mail is indispensable. But it has only been around for a fairly short time.

The ARPANET (see page 286) spawned electronic mail, or e-mail, which allows messages to be sent from one person to another across the network. Ray Tomlinson, a computer engineer for Bolt, Beranek, and Newman, the company hired to build the ARPANET, invented e-mail. Tomlinson says he invented e-mail "because it seemed like a neat idea." LOL, Ray, Thx! :)

First e-mail programs: Tomlinson wrote two electronic message programs for the ARPANET called SNDMSG for sending messages and RDMAIL for receiving them. At first, messages could only be left for others using the same computer, but Tomlinson soon found a way to adapt the programs so they could send messages on ARPANET.

First e-mail message: In 1971, Tomlinson sent the first e-mail across the ARPANET network. That first message was "QWERTYUIOP," the letters across the top of the keyboard. Not exactly "Mr. Watson, come here..." but pretty historic just the same. The first e-mail didn't have far to travel—the two computers were side-by-side on the same desk! Fast fact: The first e-mail sent by a monarch came in 1976; Queen Elizabeth of Great Britain sent congratulations to network engineers.

First use of @ sign: To determine where that very first e-mail message was going, Tomlinson chose the @ symbol, which means "at." It's been there from the beginning!

World Wide Web

The Internet began as a collection of university systems (see page 286), filled with alphabet soup including TCP, IP, Usenet, BITNET, etc. But "regular" folks could not really use the Net's world-spanning power. Then along came a guy named Tim to turn the Internet into the World Wide Web.

Mr. Web

The World Wide Web was created by Tim Berners-Lee of Great Britain in 1991. He introduced the system as a way to publish text and pictures on the Internet. A decade earlier at CERN, a Swiss physics laboratory, Berners-Lee had set up a small system that enabled scientists there to retrieve answers on their own time (answers he was tired of giving to different people over and over again!). He wrote a program called Enquire to let scientists working on different computers share information at the same time. In 1984, he decided to use Enquire to help scientists around the world, not just in Switzerland. The next big step was getting computers from different systems in different places to speak the same language.

The First Web Browser

The **first Web browser** popular with personal computer users was called Mosaic and was introduced in 1993. It was developed at the University of Illinois by a team led by a student named Marc Andreessen. Mosaic was the first browser to include graphics *and* text. Andreessen and others went on to start Netscape Communications, which launched their World Wide Web browser, called Netscape Navigator, in 1994.

First Web Code

By 1989, Berners-Lee had written the **first Web code**, called HTML (HyperText Markup Language). Each Web site on the Internet was built using HTML. He also developed software for the **first Web browser** (see the box), and the **first Web server**. A Web server stores Web pages on a computer and makes them available to others who wish to access them.

First Web Communication Language

In 1990, Berners-Lee wrote the HyperText Transfer Protocol (HTTP), the **first language computers used to communicate over the Internet**. He designed the system that gives each page an "address" so it can be located again and again. That's right: One guy created URLs (Universal Resource Locators).

First Web Site

The **first Web site**, built by Berners-Lee, was "info.cern.ch" and was first put online on August 6, 1991. The site explained what the World Wide Web was and how to use a Web server. Berners-Lee's list of Web sites then became the **first Web directory.**

"Dot's" Not All!

So much has happened in the world of the Internet and the Web that there are firsts popping up all over the place. Here are a few more:

The first registered domain name was given to Symbolics.com, registered on March 15, 1985.

The term "information superhighway," describing the Internet, was first popularized by Vice President Al Gore in 1991.

The term "surfing the Internet" was coined by Jean Armour Polly, a public librarian from upstate New York, who popularized the term in print in an article called "Surfing the Internet," published in the *Wilson Library Bulletin* in June 1992.

The first major search engine was AltaVista, created in 1995 by scientists at Digital Equipment Corporation's Research lab in Palo Alto, California. They created a system that could store every word of every page of every Web site and put it all in a fast, searchable database. AltaVista also created the first search engine with full-text translator into many different languages.

First :-)

Those little smiley faces made by typed characters are called emoticons (mixing "emotion" and "icon"). You know, :) or ;-| or :-D. Scientist Kevin McKenzie first suggested something like emoticons in 1979, but the first such face put into e-mail text occurred on September 19, 1982, by Scott Fahlman at Carnegie Mellon University. He suggested both :-) and :-(as the first symbols. By now, people have created hundreds more.

CHAPTER 13

Transportation

We covered flying in Chapter 1—now it's time to keep our feet on the ground and our keels in the water to discover some firsts about how people get from place to place.

Floating Firsts

The earliest people had an easy way to get around on land—they walked! But on the water— whether a river, lake, or ocean—they needed something to keep them from sinking. Since water wings were out of the question way back then (no plastic!), people used hundreds of different types of small boats, from kayaks and canoes to rafts and rowboats. Ancient Egyptians were the first to use sails, which caught the wind and helped boats go faster. Wooden sailing ships got larger and larger over time. But in the early 1800s, with the advent of steam and other types of engines, along with new ways of making steel and iron, new kinds of ships were created. Here are some important nautical firsts from the age of powered shipping:

1783 First practical steamboat was built by the Marquis Claude de Jouffroy d'Abbans of France.

1787 First American steamboats were built by James Fitch of Philadelphia, who got the first official steamboat licenses from Congress. Fitch's boat was a paddle wheeler using huge paddles at the back of the boat to move through the water.

1807 First passenger steamboat trips were started by Robert Fulton, on the Hudson River between Albany and New York City.

1819 First steamboat (*Savannah*) crossed the Atlantic Ocean.

1834 First iron sailing ship in the United States was the *John Randolph*, built in Georgia. All other ships of the time were made of wood.

1838 First scheduled transatlantic steamboat trips; the *Sirius* steamed from America to England.

1845 First steam-powered, iron-hulled, propeller-driven ocean liner, *Great Britain*, was launched. It was designed by Isambard Brunel of Great Britain.

1864 First boat powered by a gasoline engine was made by Étienne Lenoir in France.

1885 First gas-driven motorboat with internal engine was built by Gottlieb Daimler.

1902 First diesel engine boat was a canal boat in France.

1935 First shipping container invented by Malcolm McLaren in England. These standard-sized boxes are filled with all sorts of goods and shipped on huge container ships. (Impress your friends by knowing that a container is either 20 or 40 feet [6 or 12 m] long and 8.5 feet [2.6 m] tall.)

1953 First supertanker (*Tina Onassis*) was built to carry oil. It was twice as big as earlier tankers.

1988 First container ship built that was too big to pass through Panama Canal. The maximum number of containers on this ship was 2,170. Today, ships can carry more than 4,000! That's a lot of shoes (or toys or books or cars . . .).

The Ironclads

Until the mid-1800s, all ships were made of wood. Beginning in the 1840s, a few ships were made from iron, but it was expensive. In 1859, the French ship the *Gloire* was the first "ironclad," a wooden ship covered with iron panels. This military ship was difficult to attack. Cannonballs bounced off the sides. These metal ships changed navies forever. In 1862, the first battle between two ironclad ships was the Union *Monitor* against the Confederate *Merrimack*. This marked the start of the age of metal battleships.

Other Watery Firsts

Big ships are only one way people float around on the water. Here are some other firsts from the watercraft world:

First Polyurethane Surfboards

In Hawaii, where surfing is part of an ancient culture, surfboards were made of wood from only three trees: ulu, koa, and wiliwili. Following World War II, which had helped create many scientific innovations, plastic technology improved tremendously. In 1946, Pete Peterson and Brant Goldsworthy made the first fiberglass surfboard. Many others contributed to shaping the modern surfboard, but the big switch from heavy wood to lightweight fiberglass helped surfing spread quickly. Not only were the new boards easier to carry, they were less expensive. Hang ten, dudes!

First Nuclear Icebreaker

Smashing through the ice, in a giant iron ship, over the poles we go, breaking through the bergs! The first nuclear-powered icebreaker, the *Lenin*, was built in 1959 by the Soviet Union. These ships helped expand exploration of the polar regions.

First Hovercraft

Hovercraft ride on a cushion of air, skimming the waves on their huge, inflatable rubber hulls. They can ride more smoothly in rough waters than traditional ships. *SRN1*, constructed in England in 1959, was the first hovercraft ever built. The concept had been invented four years earlier by Christopher Cockerell. By 1962, there was regular hovercraft passenger service in England.

First Windsurfers

A combination of sailing and surfing, windsurfing has become a popular pastime on oceans and lakes. The first popular sailboards were made by Hoyle Schweitzer and James Drake of the United States in 1968. They built an industry and trademarked the name Windsurfer. But they did not make the first sailboards. That honor goes to Peter Chilvers of Britain, who made one in 1958 when he was 12! Another man, Newman Darby, made one in 1964 and actually wrote about it in a science magazine.

First Boogie Boards

California surfer Tom Morey shaped the first bodyboard, which he called a "boogie board," out of Styrofoam in 1971. Boogie boards are perfect for kids to use on smaller waves closer to shore.

First Jet Skis

To the joy of speed fans and the annoyance of those who enjoy silence, Jet Skis were invented in 1973 by Clayton Jacobsen of the Kawasaki Corp. Combining the speed and handling of motorcycles with the fun of being on the water, Jet Skis kicked off a new wave of motorized "personal watercraft" of all shapes and sizes.

Cycling into First

You and your, well, seat should say thanks to John Starley every time you sit on your bicycle. Before Starley came along to perfect the chain drive and design a "modern" bike, bikes looked—and felt—very different. One kind of early bike had a huge front wheel, a hard seat, and solid wood tires. Try bouncing over pavement on that bike, called—ouch—a boneshaker! Here are some cycling firsts:

1790 Count de Sivrac of France created an early form of bicycle, called the *célérifère* (wheeled horse). It was a frame with two wheels. The rider simply walked while sitting on the frame.

1817 German Baron Karl von Drais made the *draisenne*, another form of the frame with wheels that was a bit more comfortable.

1839 Kirkpatrick Macmillan of Scotland built the first bicycle with pedals. It had iron wheels and no chain.

1861 Pierre Michaux created the first rotary pedal bike—this was the boneshaker! The spinning pedals made it easier to push them.

MY FIRST...

I first rode on a tricycle when I was _____ years old.

My first bike with training wheels was _____ [color].

I was _____ years old when I first rode without training wheels. The first place I ever rode my bike without training wheels was _____

_____.

Birth of BMX

While road bikes are fine for Lance Armstrong, it's BMX bikes—smaller wheels, thicker frames, fewer gears—for many kids in America and around the world. BMX (which stands, sort of, for bicycle motocross) is modeled after a form of motorcycle racing. In BMX, racers speed around short dirt tracks, hopping over mounds of earth or rattling across rugged ground. California rider Scot Breithaupt is known as the Father of BMX. In 1970, he built the first track for BMX riders, and that November held the first "official" BMX races. In recent years, stunt bike riding, as seen in the X Games and other places, has evolved out of BMX racing.

1870 James Starley invented the *Penny Farthing*, a bike with a huge front wheel. The riders were as much as eight feet (2 m) above the ground. Don't fall!

1879 H. J. Lawson invented first bike that used a chain to drive one of the wheels.

1885 The Rover model, designed by John Starley (James's nephew), set a new standard. The model's frame, handlebars, and seat looked much like those on bikes of today.

1888 First inflatable bike tires were created by John Dunlop.

1903 First Tour de France was won by Maurice Garin of France. This monthlong race became the most famous long-distance competition in the world.

1979 Gary Fisher started the first mountain-bike company in Colorado. Mountain bikes use rugged tires and smaller frames to let riders go "off-road" more easily and safely.

Starting Cars

Starting cars, get it? You use a key to start a car and we're talking about how cars started . . . okay, sorry. So, who invented the car? Like many inventions, it was the result of hard work by many people.

In 1862, Étienne Lenoir of France created the **first gasoline engine**. He attached it to a horse carriage (without the horse!) and made a journey of 12 miles (19 km), the first ever in a gas-powered vehicle. But Lenoir wanted to build motorboats, not cars, and did not continue work on the automobile.

In 1876, American George Selden received the **first patent for an internal-combustion engine** mounted on the typical carriage of the times (usually drawn by horses; this led to an early nickname for the car: "horseless carriage"). However, it was never built.

In 1885, Karl Benz of Germany was the **first to combine a gas engine with a frame and wheels to make a motor car**. His first car (left) had only three wheels. In 1888, he became the first car salesman when he sold one of his three-wheel cars to Frenchman Emile Roger.

In 1891, Emile Levassor of France was the **first person to put four wheels on his automobile**. He also put the engine at the front of the car, setting up the basic model for most future cars.

In 1891, Charles Duryea became the **first American carmaker**. He built his first automobile in 1891, and started selling cars in 1896 in Springfield, Massachusetts. Here's a cool fact: Duryea made the first armored car in 1898.

In 1899, Random Olds built the **first car factory in America** in Detroit, Michigan. And, yes, he made Oldsmobiles.

In 1908, pioneer automaker Henry Ford (see page 304) released the first of his Model T cars, the **first mass-produced automobile**.

Safety First!

As people climbed into these metal boxes and started speeding around, government officials had to come up with ways to keep everyone safe. Here are some auto safety milestones:

First gaslight traffic light: London, 1868

First traffic accident: London, 1897

First person arrested for speeding in America: Jacob German, near New York City, 1899—for going 12 miles (19 km) per hour!

First electric traffic lights: Paris, 1900

First three-point lap and shoulder belt: In Volvo cars, 1958, invented by Nils Bohlin of Sweden

First country to make wearing seat belts mandatory by law: Czechoslovakia, 1969

First car air bags: Some American cars, 1974

First antilock brakes: Some German cars, 1982

Riding Around Town

Many people get around using some form of public transportation, from buses and subways to taxis and trolleys. The idea of a vehicle traveling on a regular route picking up passengers and delivering them to a series of "stops" was developed in 1662 by philosopher and writer Blaise Pascal in Paris. As cities got bigger and bigger, the idea of moving many people at one time became more and more important; transportation technology made this both faster and safer. A wide variety of vehicles was used for this purpose. Now, where did I put my bus pass?

First bus service: In 1825, horse-drawn carriages carried large numbers of people between several cities in Great Britain.

First American streetcar service: Horse-drawn cars ran on rails in the streets of New York City, beginning in 1825. The first car in this service was named the John Mason, and the first driver was a fellow named Lank O'Dell.

First elevated railway: In 1867, a railroad started whizzing above New York City streets on a trestle track.

First San Francisco cable car: The famous cable cars first started riding the steep hills of San Francisco in 1873. A ride cost five cents.

First gasoline buses: Hermann Golze made the first buses in Germany in 1895.

First taxi service: Hermann Dütz put meters on automobiles for the first time in 1896 in Stuttgart, Germany. Riders could hire these "taxis" and pay for the distance of their ride. Electric taxis were first used in Philadelphia later that year.

First subway: The world's first subway (an underground railroad) opened in London in 1863. America's first was the Tremont Street Subway in Boston, in 1895. The first New York City subway, in 1904, was the IRT (Interborough Rapid Transit), which ran in Manhattan and cost a nickel to ride.

The First Yellow Bus

Getting to school wasn't always as easy as it is today. Pretty much everyone walked to the first schools, then some hopped into horse-drawn wagons, and then into large automobiles after they were invented. School buses of various shapes and sizes were developed in the years after World War I. As more and more buses hit the highways, the government, concerned for student safety, passed some rules. And so, in 1939, the National Conference on School Transportation decided that school buses should be painted a bright color to make them visible to all drivers. They chose a color called National School Bus Yellow (really!). See if *your* bus driver knows that!

More Car Firsts!

Since there are more cars in America than people—believe it or not—we thought cars deserved even more pages of firsts.

First woman to drive a car in America: Genevra Mudge in an electric car in 1898

First drive across country in reverse: Charles Creighton and James Hargis backed up from New York to Los Angeles in 1930. And no, we don't know why they did this.

First public parking garage in America: Opened in Boston, Massachusetts, in 1899

First mobile home: Designed in 1929 by Glenn Curtiss, whom you might remember for his many aviation firsts (see Chapter 1)

First parking meter: Installed in Oklahoma City, Oklahoma, in 1935; the cost was five cents for a parking space for the entire day.

First car-airplane combo: The Arrowbile, built by the Waterman Arrowplane Corp. in Santa Monica, California, in 1939. It could both fly and drive on the highway.

First car with air conditioning: The 1939 Packard

First Volkswagen Beetle: Built in Germany in 1949

First Hot Wheels toy cars:

Sixteen models were first sold by Mattel in 1968.

First solar-powered car race: 1985 Tour de Sol in Switzerland; in 1990, the first annual Sunrayce across America was held among student-made solar-powered cars.

First car to break the sound barrier on land: In 1979, Stan Barrett drove the Budweiser Rocket 739.666 miles (1,190.38 km) per hour, or Mach 1.01, in the California desert.

First vehicles powered by natural gas: In 1992, Southern California Gas Co. used trucks powered by natural gas.

First electric car sold to the public: EV-1, introduced in America in 1996

IN THE FIRST PLACE...

Henry Ford

Henry Ford was not the first man to make cars in America, but he was the first to make cars that everyone in America could afford to buy. Ford's innovation came in the method he used to make cars. In 1913, he created the first assembly line ever installed in a factory. It simply revolutionized manufacturing and, in many ways, America.

An engineer by training, he founded the Ford Motor Company in 1903. While many companies were making cars of all types in the first decade of the 20th century, Ford recognized that making cars quickly and inexpensively would be the way to reach the

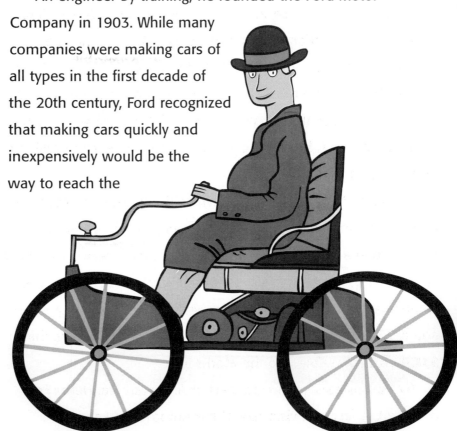

greatest number of customers. He created the Model T and began selling it in 1908. He designed the car so that it could be put together with a standard set of parts, making it fairly simple to build. However, he wanted a way he could work even faster.

In 1913, inspired by a variety of factory innovations, he created the first assembly line in the world. A Model T under construction on this line moved along a conveyor belt. As it passed by 84 different stations, workers added different parts. Using this method, instead of producing only several cars a day, Ford's factory could produce a complete car in less than 90 minutes. With these assembly lines in enormous factories, Ford churned out cars at an amazing pace. By 1918, half the cars in America were Model Ts. The first Model Ts sold for $850, a lot of money then, but not a fortune (a teacher's average annual salary was about $800 in those days, for example). Amazingly, by 1925, Ford had lowered the price to $290, well within reach of millions of American families.

Thanks to the growth in car ownership, spurred by Model Ts, new roads were built. Thanks to the roads, new businesses sprang up in a host of industries, many of them created to service all those new cars: gas stations, supermarkets, road construction companies, hotels, restaurants, car-parts makers, and on and on and on. The Sears Roebuck catalog in 1920 featured more than 5,000 products relating to the Model T.

By making cars an integral part of American life, Henry Ford became the first true visionary of the Automobile Age.

Motorcycle Firsts

You can't ride one yet, but don't you sometimes wish you could? Motorcycles are so sleek-looking: plated in shiny metal, enhanced with wicked accessories, and powered by a growling engine. As we roll along through transportation firsts, let's take a walk on the wild side and discover some motorcycle firsts:

The idea of adding an engine to a bicycle came up almost as soon as people had bicycles. In 1868, William Austin of Massachusetts made the ***first motorcycle*** by putting a small steam engine onto a bicycle frame. It wasn't very powerful, though, because the engine had to be so small. The search continued. . . .

Motorcycles really kicked into gear in Germany among the gas-engine pioneers. In 1885, Gottlieb Daimler, who later became an important carmaker, looked at a gas-powered internal

Scooter Central

In many cities in Europe and Asia, it's not motorcycles or cars or even bikes that you see filling up traffic lanes: It's scooters. Not as powerful as motorcycles but motorized to be faster than bikes, scooters are fun to ride, easy to park, and, well, they look really cool. The first scooter was similar to the first motorcycle (see 1885 above). The 1902 *autofauteuil*, made in France by Georges Gauthier, introduced a new kind of design, with a step-through frame, a long rectangular seat, and a short windshield beneath the handlebars. Scooters evolved from there. A key step was the first Vespa scooter, made in 1946 by Enrico Piaggio's Italian company. Vespas quickly became the most popular models in the world and continue to sell millions of scooters in dozens of countries, including the United States.

first gear

Motor vehicles are driven by engines. The engines are controlled with devices called gears, which determine how fast the engine parts revolve, helping to increase or decrease speed. Engines have to start someplace, and the place they start is called "first gear." Motors go slowest in first gear; as a rider wants to speed up, he moves up in gears. Motorcycles usually have four gears, while cars can often have five, plus reverse gear. Drivers use a gearshift lever or handle to switch between the vehicle's gears.

combustion engine invented by Nicolas Otto. Daimler mounted it to a bicycle frame, creating the ***first gasoline-powered motorcycle***.

The ***first American-made motorcycle*** was produced in 1901 by Hendee Manufacturing Company in Springfield, Massachusetts. Their "Indian" model remains one of the most famous motorcycles of all time.

Motorcycles are great for long trips, as George Wyman discovered in 1903 when he became the ***first person to ride a motorcycle across the United States***.

Perhaps the most famous motorcycles in the world were first made in 1903. That year, William Harley and Arthur and Walter Davidson made the ***first Harley-Davidson motorcycles***.

In 1949, Hondas became the ***first Japanese motorcycles***. Fast and reliable, they became big sellers in the United States.

Motorcycles call for extra protection. In 1966, Georgia became the ***first state to make helmets mandatory for all riders***.

Trains

We'll call this section "the caboose" on our transportation train—and, hey, look, it's all about trains! Trains were the first real rapid transportation. Their invention helped power the Industrial Revolution in Europe and helped create the Western United States by allowing movement of people and goods rapidly into new areas. Though not as important today—thanks to cars and trucks—trains remain a part of travel in just about every country. Here are some key train firsts:

1804 First steam locomotive was built by Richard Trevithick in England.

1807 The Oystermouth Railway in Wales was the first to carry passengers.

1823 John Stevens was granted the first charter for a steam-powered railroad in America; he called it the Pennsylvania Railroad when it opened in 1829.

Steaming Ahead

The big idea that made trains possible was steam power. But that idea was actually thousands of years old. An ancient Roman named Ctesibus, living in Egypt, used it to make a globe spin around in about 200 BCE. Many inventors used steam to power various devices, but it took a Scotsman named James Watt to make all those ideas work together. In 1774, he unveiled the first working, practical steam engine.

1828 The first railroad in the United States with regularly scheduled service was the Baltimore & Ohio Railroad. It started out using horse-drawn cars on rails.

1830 The B&O's first steam locomotive was called *Tom Thumb*. It was the first locomotive used to pull passengers in America.

1859 Train travel could sometimes take several days; in this year, the Pullman Company created the first "sleeper" cars, complete with beds for passengers to sleep in. By 1865, the sleepers had been improved with carpeting, furnaces, and fancy furniture.

1867 Trains became vital in moving food from farms to cities. This year, the creation of the refrigerator car helped preserve fruits and vegetables for long-distance travel.

1868 People on trains gotta eat, too! The first dining car was called the "Delmonico," named for a New York City restaurant.

1869 This is one of the most important dates in American history. For the first time, a railroad linked the East and West Coasts of the American continent when the Union Pacific tracks met the Central Pacific tracks at Promontory Point, Utah.

1879 There is more to trains than steam. The first electric train was demonstrated by Werner von Siemens of Germany.

1921 The first diesel locomotive went into regular operation in Tunisia.

1965 The first "bullet train," going more than 100 miles (160 km) per hour, started in Tokaido, Japan.

Index

The Page of Lasts

As we wrap up the Scholastic Book of Firsts, we'll use our final page to take a look at some interesting lasts. We've spent the entire book talking about things that came first; on this page, we'll skip right to the end. Here are some historic lasts:

Last Bare-Knuckle Boxing Match

Since the time of the ancient Greeks, the sport of boxing was done with bare hands. New rules created by England's marquis of Queensberry in the late 1800s added boxing gloves and timed rounds. The last fight without gloves was in 1889, when John L. Sullivan defeated fellow American Jake Kilrain in 75 rounds!

Last Czar of Russia

Following the Russian Revolution in 1917, Nicholas II lost his position as the czar of Russia, becoming the last man to hold this title. The first czar was Ivan the Terrible in 1547.

Last Person to Catch Smallpox

Ali Maow Maalin, a native of Somalia, caught the dreaded disease known as smallpox in 1977. Because of a worldwide program to inoculate people against this deadly disease, Maalin was the final person to catch it. He survived.

Last Flight of the Concorde

On October 24, 2003, the needle-nosed plane called the Concorde touched down for the final time in London. Since 1969, the jet had zoomed faster than any other type of commercial plane.